Using the 6800 Microprocessor

by

Elmer Poe

Howard W. Sams & Co., Inc.
4300 WEST 62ND ST. INDIANAPOLIS, INDIANA 46268 USA

FIRST EDITION
FIRST PRINTING—1978

International Standard Book Number: 0-672-21512-8
Library of Congress Catalog Card Number: 77-93168

Printed in the United States of America.

Preface

The 6800 microprocessor has become very popular since its introduction. It has a straightforward internal architecture, a powerful and efficient instruction set, and sophisticated support devices. As it is used in increasingly diverse applications its potential users are unlikely to be familiar with it. The text that follows will acquaint the reader with the hardware and software of the 6800 by guiding the reader through the conception, configuration, writing, and running of a variety of programs that demonstrate practical use of a 6800 system. Hardware considerations are emphasized in the implementation of the programs. Any 6800-based system from a bare bones homebrew to a fully expanded microcomputer can run the programs developed. The reader needs no special background in digital electronics to use this book or a 6800. It is a fun machine, so read on and enjoy.

ELMER POE

Contents

CHAPTER 14

CHAPTER 15

APPENDIX

CHAPTER 1

Welcome to the 6800

Microprocessors are revolutionizing the world of electronics. They are appearing in everything from microwave ovens to automobile ignitions, from glass furnaces to video games. These extraordinary devices are proliferating in applications traditionally dominated by analog devices. The 6800, introduced in 1974, is popular among designers because it is easy to use, extremely versatile, and fun to use.

Objectives

You will be able to:

1. Sketch the block diagram of a 6800 processor
2. Explain the operation of the data bus and R/W line
3. Explain the flow of data in a simple processor

A microprocessor is a digital integrated circuit that can perform a task by following a series of instructions given it by a programmer. That group of instructions that a processor can execute is its instruction set. The 6800 instruction set has 72 separate instructions including arithmetic, logic, decision making, and internal housekeeping instructions. Those instructions that a processor must perform to accomplish a task are called a program. The processor executes a program by executing the instructions sequentially as they appear in the program listing. The great power of a microprocessor lies in its programmability; to change its function only the program must be changed.

The instructions and all of the data used by a processor are presented to it and handled by it in digital form. A processor deals with information not as single digital bits but in groups of bits called words. Common word sizes are 4, 8, and 16 bits but the most widely used processors, including the 6800, are 8-bit machines. An 8-bit word, usually called a byte, has 8 bits in parallel that are dealt with as a single entity; 0101 1100, 0000 0100, and 0101 0101 are three bytes that could be handled by a processor.

Implementing the logic required by the 6800 requires a great amount of space on an IC. The small amount of excess space available for memory is usually reserved for use by the processor. As a result of this space crunch, the program's instructions and data must be stored on a separate chip. (Recent advances in the fabrication of ICs make a chip possible that includes the processor and some user-accessible memory.) The program's instruction and data flow to and from the processor over the data bus is a group of 8 lines that connects the processor to memory and other peripheral devices. Since data can flow either into or out of the processor over the same 8 lines, the data bus is called bidirectional. The data bus lines are designated D0–D7; D0 is the least significant line, D7 is the most significant line. The direction of data flow on the bus is indicated by the condition of one of the control lines, the read/write line. Connecting the processor and memory, the R/W line is usually controlled by the processor. When it makes the R/W high, the processor expects to transfer information from memory into itself, a process called reading from memory. When the R/W line is low, the processor expects to transfer information to memory, called writing to memory.

Associated with the data bus is the address bus. Since all of the program's instructions are stored on one chip, the processor must be able to tell the memory chip exactly which instruction it wants to execute. Fig. 1-1 shows how this is accomplished.

The 6810 is a random access memory that contains 128 bytes. The data bus allows the transfer of data and the R/W line de-

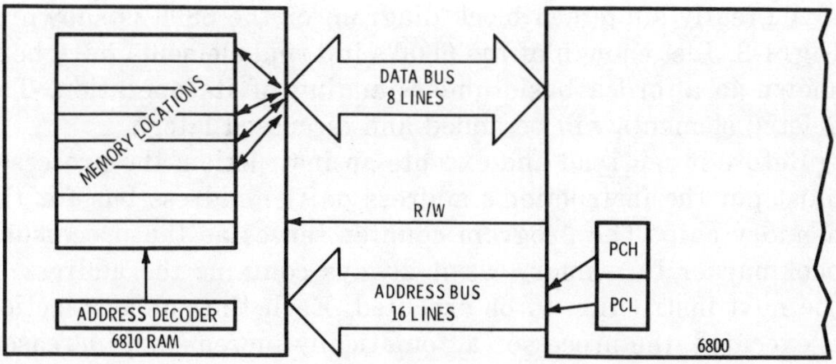

Fig. 1-1. Memory addressing.

termines the direction of that transfer. Each byte in the 6810 is internally assigned a number, called an address. When the address, in binary, of a particular byte is presented to the 6810's address decoder circuit, the contents of that address, a byte of information, is placed at the data bus. The other 127 bytes are kept off the data bus. While the selected byte is at the data bus, a read or write operation with the processor may be performed. The processor must, then, specify the address of any instruction it wants. It does this via the address bus.

The address of the byte desired is placed on the address bus, decoded by the RAM circuitry, and the requested byte is placed at the data bus. The address bus is not bidirectional, only the processor puts out addresses. Notice that the address bus is 2 bytes, 16 bits, wide. If it were one byte wide the processor could access only 256 bytes of memory, enough for simple programs but not enough for more sophisticated ones which may require thousands of bytes. Since the address bus is two bytes wide

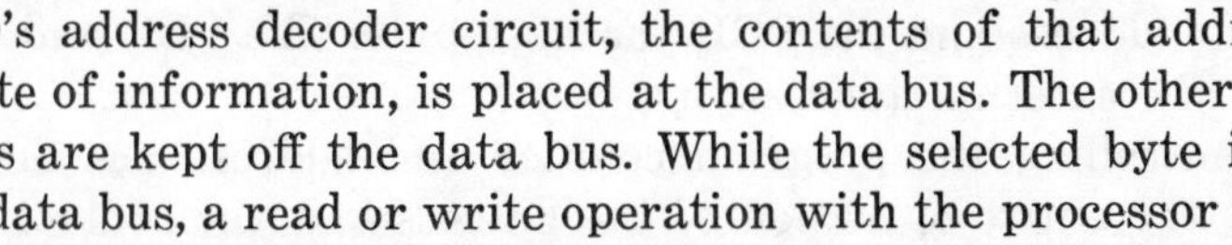

Fig. 1-2. The address bus.

the 6800 can directly access any one of 65,535 bytes, often referred to as 64K. The least significant 8 bits are referred to as the low address byte; the most significant 8 bits are the high address byte. The address bits are numbered A0–A15; A0 being the least significant and A15 the most significant. The address line organization is shown in Fig. 1-2.

A greatly simplified block diagram of the 6800 is shown in Fig. 1-3. Just enough of the 6800's internal elements have been shown to afford a basic understanding of its operation. The deleted elements will be added and discussed later.

Before it can read and execute an instruction, the processor must put the instruction's address on the address bus for the memory chip. The program counter serves as the processor's bookmarker in memory, as it always contains the address of the next instruction to be executed. Each time an instruction is executed, the processor automatically increments, increases, the program counter so that it again contains the address of the next instruction. Incrementing the program counter is relatively simple since the instructions of a program are normally stored and executed sequentially. The program counter is a two-byte storage unit in the processor designated PCL and PCH. The PCL contains the low byte of the next instruction's address and the PCH the high byte. The PCL and PCH feed the external address bus.

Controlling the program counter and address bus and, in fact, the entire operation of the processor is the control unit. The control unit is the brain of the processor. Notice in Fig. 1-3 that the control unit is connected to every other block in the processor. A relatively easy way to demonstrate the control unit's function as well as that of the other internal registers is to follow the processor through the execution of some instructions.

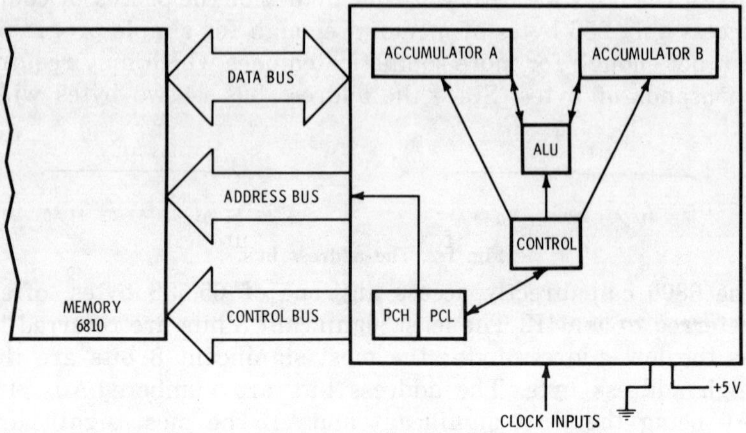

Fig. 1-3. Simplified block diagram of the 6800.

The control unit initiates an instruction fetch and decode in which it directs the program counter to put its contents on the address bus and at the same time pulls the R/W line high indicating a read from memory operation. The byte that is transferred from memory over the data bus is an instruction. The control unit evaluates the incoming byte and determines the operation to be performed and then increments the program counter.

Some instructions simply move data from memory to the processor. For these instructions the processor must determine the address of the data to be moved and put that address onto the address bus while setting up the data bus for a read operation. When the data is transferred into the processor it usually is placed in either Accumulator A or Accumulator B. ACCA and ACCB are 8-bit temporary storage registers in the processor that are controlled by the program. The accumulators are essential since arithmetic and logic instructions generally must be performed in the processor. They serve, then, as places in the processor to store data temporarily.

Some instructions cause an arithmetic or logic function, perhaps addition, to be performed on data stored in both an accumulator and in memory. These instructions are performed in the arithmetic logic unit (alu). The control unit tells the alu the location of the data and the operation to be performed. The alu simply does the operation called for, it does not store or hold data. The result of an alu operation is usually automatically returned to an accumulator. After data has been loaded into the processor and modified it is placed back in memory with another instruction. The cycle of bringing data into the processor, modifying it and then storing it is common and frequently used in every program.

The processor is always guided by the control unit which is, in turn, always under program control. In dedicated systems, systems that always perform the same function, e.g., a processor controlled automobile carburetion system, the program is stored in read only memory (ROM). Read only memory is nonvolatile, nonchangeable memory; it remembers even when the power is off. Varying data, manifold temperature, and pressure in the carburetor example is stored in RAM.

The 6800 is available today in a wide variety of configurations ranging from simple systems for less than $200 to sophisticated microcomputer systems for more than $200. Generally the higher priced units have a larger power supply and more memory. This book is usable with the least expensive system, the most expensive system, or any system in between.

CHAPTER 2

Decimal, Hexadecimal, and Binary Systems

The 6800 is a microprocessor, a small computer. Like other computers the 6800 deals only in binary numbers. Eight-bit binary numbers, bytes, are awkward to read, write, and use so industry generally represents the 8-bit binaries in hexadecimal form. To use the 6800 efficiently you should be comfortable with the binary and hexadecimal systems.

Objectives

You will be able to:

1. Perform binary to decimal and decimal to binary conversions
2. Perform hexadecimal to decimal and decimal to hexadecimal conversions
3. Perform binary to hexadecimal and hexadecimal to binary conversions

The binary and hexadecimal systems are much like the decimal system. You are probably so used to the decimal system that you do not think about its basic organization. It has only 10 completely unique characters, 0, 1, 2, 3, 4, 5, 6, 7, 8, and 9. The counting sequence begins at 0 and proceeds to 9 with each character representing one more than the last. To represent one more than 9 two characters must be used, 10. The one indicates that the entire system has been used one time, the zero indicates that it was exactly one time. One more than 10 is 11. The most significant 1 represents one complete pass through the system, the least significant 1 indicates that the total count is one more than 10, 11 which is usually called eleven. The physical positions of the numbers in the decimal system represent the powers of 10 as shown in Fig. 2-1. The value of any decimal

10^4	10^3	10^2	10^1	10^0
10000's	1000's	100's	10's	1's
	4	3	6	5

Fig. 2-1. Powers of 10.

number can be determined by using Fig. 2-1. Consider 4365, which can be broken into powers of 10 from Fig. 2-1.

$$\begin{aligned} 4 \times 1000 &= 4000 \\ 3 \times 100 &= 300 \\ 6 \times 10 &= 60 \\ 5 \times 1 &= 5 \\ & \overline{\overline{4365}} \end{aligned}$$

Using Fig. 2-1 to determine the value of a number seems trivial but the same technique can be used in the binary system. The binary system has only two unique characters, 0 and 1. All numbers must be represented by combinations of them. The binary count begins at zero and progresses to one. At this point both of the unique characters have been used. One more than one must be represented as 10. Just as in the decimal system each number place represents a power of two. These powers of two and their decimal equivalents are shown in Fig. 2-2.

2^7	2^6	2^5	2^4	2^3	2^2	2^1	2^0
128	64	32	16	8	4	2	1

Fig. 2-2. Powers of 2.

10 in binary is:

$$
\begin{array}{r}
1 \times 2 = 2 \\
0 \times 1 = \underline{0} \\
\overline{\overline{2}} \text{ decimal}
\end{array}
$$

101 in binary is:

$$
\begin{array}{r}
1 \times 4 = 4 \\
0 \times 2 = 0 \\
1 \times 1 = \underline{1} \\
\overline{\overline{5}} \text{ decimal}
\end{array}
$$

1001 0110 in binary is:

$$
\begin{array}{rrr}
1 \times & 128 = & 128 \\
0 \times & 64 = & 0 \\
0 \times & 32 = & 0 \\
1 \times & 16 = & 16 \\
0 \times & 8 = & 0 \\
1 \times & 4 = & 4 \\
1 \times & 2 = & 2 \\
0 \times & 1 = & \underline{0} \\
 & & \overline{\overline{150}} \text{ decimal}
\end{array}
$$

Any binary number can be expressed in decimal form using Fig. 2-2. Decimal numbers can be expressed in binary using about the same process. The decimal number is divided by the largest power of 2 that is equal to or smaller than the decimal number. See Fig. 2-3. Decimal 7 is divided by 4, the largest

$$
\begin{array}{l}
4\overline{)7} = 1 \\
-4 \qquad\qquad\qquad 1 \quad 1 \quad 1 \\
2\overline{)3} = 1 \\
-2 \\
1\overline{)1} = 1 \\
\underline{-1} \\
\ \ 0
\end{array}
$$

Fig. 2-3. Decimal to binary conversion.

power of 2 that will divide into 7. A 1 is put in the 4's position and the remainder, 3, is divided by 2, the largest power that will divide into 3. A 1 is put into the 2's position and the remainder, 1, is divided by 1, the only binary position left. A 1 is recorded in the 1's place. Since the remainder of the last division is zero the conversion is complete. Decimal 7 is 111 in binary.

Decimal 27 is:

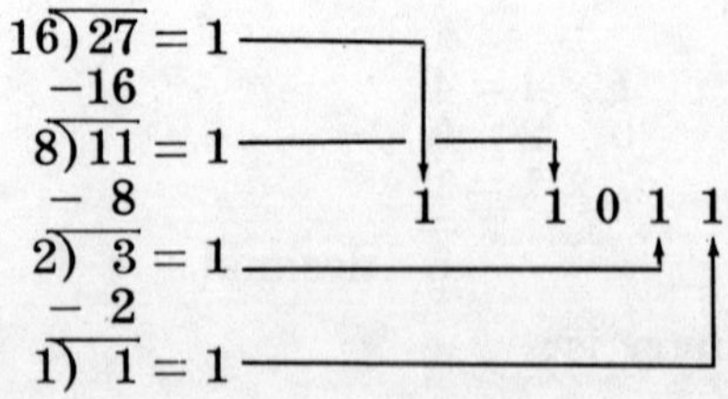

Notice the zero recorded in the 2^2, or 4's, position. It indicates that no division by 4 was performed.

Decimal 44 is:

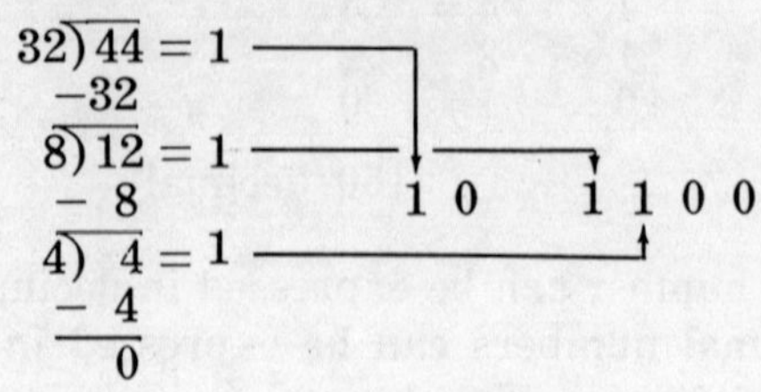

The zeros have again been added to indicate that no division by 16, 2, or 1 was performed.

The hexadecimal system has 16 unique characters, 0, 1, 2, 3, 4, 5, 6, 7, 8, 9, A, B, C, D, E, and F. A through F represent values of 10 through 15. The hex count begins at 0 and increases to F. One more than F is indicated by 10. The powers of 16 and their decimal equivalents are shown in Fig. 2-4.

Any hexadecimal number can be expressed in decimal form using Fig. 2-4. Each digit is multiplied by its power of 16 and all of those products are added.

F4 hex is:

16^3	16^2	16^1	16^0
4096	256	16	1

Fig. 2-4. Powers of 16.

$$
\begin{array}{rcrl}
F(15) \times & 16 = & 240 & \\
4 \times & 1 = & 4 & \\
\hline\hline
 & & 244 & \text{decimal}
\end{array}
$$

7E6 hex is:

$$
\begin{array}{rcrl}
7 \times & 256 = & 1792 & \\
E(14) \times & 16 = & 224 & \\
6 \times & 1 = & 6 & \\
\hline\hline
 & & 2022 & \text{decimal}
\end{array}
$$

32 hex is:

$$
\begin{array}{rcrl}
3 \times & 16 = & 48 & \\
2 \times & 1 = & 2 & \\
\hline\hline
 & & 50 & \text{decimal}
\end{array}
$$

Notice that the hex number 32 does not represent the same quantity as the decimal 32.

Decimal to hex conversions are performed using the process used in decimal to binary conversion. The decimal number is divided by the largest power of 16 that is smaller than the decimal. The answer is placed in that power of 16's position and the remainder is divided by the largest power of 16 that is smaller than the remainder. The conversion is completed when the remainder is zero.

Decimal 79 is:

$$
\begin{array}{rl}
16\overline{)79} = 4 & \rightarrow \\
-64 & \\
1\overline{)15} = F(15) & \rightarrow \quad 4F \text{ Hexadecimal} \\
-15 & \\
\hline
0 &
\end{array}
$$

Decimal 486 is:

$$
\begin{array}{rl}
256\overline{)486} = 1 & \rightarrow \\
-256 & \qquad 1\ E\ 6 \quad \text{Hexadecimal} \\
16\overline{)230} = E(14) & \rightarrow \\
-224 & \\
1\overline{)\ \ 6} = 6 & \rightarrow \\
-6 & \\
\hline
0 &
\end{array}
$$

Decimal 27562 is:

```
4096)27562 = 6 ─────────┐
    -24576              │
256)  2986 = B(11) ─────┼─┐
     -2816              6 B A A   Hexadecimal
16)    170 = A(10) ─────────┘ │
      -160                    │
1)      10 = A(10) ───────────┘
       -10
         0
```

Perhaps the easiest conversions are those from hex to binary and binary to hex. The unique hex characters and their binary counterparts are listed in Fig. 2-5. Notice that any single hex can be represented by one four-bit binary number. Hex to

Hex	Binary
0	0000
1	0001
2	0010
3	0011
4	0100
5	0101
6	0110
7	0111
8	1000
9	1001
A	1010
B	1011
C	1100
D	1101
E	1110
F	1111

Fig. 2-5. Hex characters and their binary counterparts.

binary conversions are performed by listing the four place binary equivalents of each hex number, 84A hex is:

```
1000   0100   1010   binary
 \/     \/     \/
 8      4      A
```

Each hex digit must be represented by four binary digits; zeros cannot be omitted.

DO hexadecimal is:

```
1101  0000  binary
 \/    \/
 D     0
```

Binary to hex conversions are easily performed. The binary number is divided into four digit groups and each group is represented by a hex character.
1010 1110 binary is:

```
  A     E    hexadecimal
 /\    /\
1010  1110
```

110 0110 binary is:

```
   6      6    hexadecimal
  /\     /\
(0)110  0110
```

Understanding the binary, hex, and decimal systems is the first important step in using a 6800 microprocessor.

CHAPTER 3

Processor Languages

Perhaps the most important part of any microprocessor system is the program that controls the behavior of the system. Many ways of expressing programs exist, and each set of symbols that can be used is called a language. To be a successful processor user, you must master one or more languages.

Objectives

You will be able to:

1. List major differences among machine, assembly, and the Basic languages
2. Use the programmer's reference card
3. Use the programming sheet
4. Assemble a simple program

The 6800 understands only binary numbers. It can recognize about 150 different binary numbers as representing executable instructions. These numbers, called op codes, make up the machine language. Very few programs are written in machine language because people don't naturally think in binary. Fig. 3-1 shows the machine language program for the addition of two numbers, A and B.

Hex	Binary
96	1001 0110
00	0000 0000
9B	1001 1011
01	0000 0001
97	1001 0111
02	0000 0010

Fig. 3-1. Addition in machine language.

The machine language's only advantage, absolute control of program content and length, is retained in assembly language. Assembly language replaces the op codes with mnemonics that describe the operations. Examples include ADDA for the addition operation and JMP for the jump operation. Programs can be written faster and easier in assembly language since it more closely resembles conversational English. Assembly language is widely used by industrial programmers. However, the processor cannot understand mnemonics and a program written in mnemonics must be assembled, or converted, into machine language. The assembly process can be carried out by hand or by a special assembler program. In Fig. 3-2 the addition program of Fig. 3-1 is written in assembly language.

```
LDDA
A
ADDA
B
STAA
C
```

Fig. 3-2. Addition in assembly language.

Although it is popular, assembly language does not allow easy solution of algebraic problems since the 6800 has only addition and subtraction functions. Because the programmer must develop even simple math functions, assembly language is called a low-level language.

The high-level programming languages were designed to overcome the math deficiencies of assembly language. Several high level languages are being used on processors but BASIC is the most widely used. BASIC statements closely resemble commonly used algebraic expressions. Fig. 3-3 shows the addition example written in BASIC.

```
LET    C = A + B
```

Fig. 3-3. Addition in BASIC.

BASIC's major disadvantage lies in the programmer's loss of program control at the machine language level. BASIC statements cannot be understood by the 6800 so they are converted, or compiled, into machine language by a compiler program. A BASIC statement may be compiled into 50 or more machine language instructions. There is usually more than one way to perform a function but the compiler knows only one of them. In time or memory sensitive programs BASIC may not produce the most efficient machine language code. A programmer working in assembly language may be able to perform the same function with one-third fewer instructions. In some applications assembly language can be more desirable than BASIC. Several versions of BASIC are available for use on processors. Differences lie in the amount of memory the compiler program requires and the number of functions available. Generally a BASIC compiler that requires less memory offers fewer functions. Current versions run from Tiny BASIC, that requires only 2K of memory but does not allow either floating or fixed point math, to full blown BASIC that requires 8K of memory and allows sophisticated functions to be performed.

Because it is a good compromise between higher and lower level languages, because it can be used on any 6800 system, and because it will allow you to become intimately knowledgeable of your system, assembly language will be used in the chapters that follow.

Remove and examine the programmer's card immediately preceding the back cover. The card can be removed by carefully cutting the inside edge. Every machine level operation that the 6800 is capable of is listed in the leftmost column of this card. Look at the first operation listed on the card, the add. ADDA is the standard 6800 mnemonic for the add operation. A 6800 assembly language program written for any system will use the mnemonics listed on the card. The op codes, representing the instructions, are found in the addressing modes columns. Ad-

Op	Assem-bly	Op	Assem-bly	Op	Assem-bly	Op	Assem-bly
0C	CLC		LDAA		LDX		LDAB
B6	LDAA		LDAB		DEX		NEGA
B9	ADCA		ABA		BGT		ADDA
B7	STAA		STAA		NOP		TAB

Fig. 3-4. Assembling simple programs.

dressing modes will be discussed in Chapter 4. How the operation is accomplished is shown in the Boolean/Arithmetic Operation column. Each letter refers to either an internal register or an external memory location. $A + M \rightarrow A$ indicates that the contents of accumulator A will be added to the contents of memory location M and the result will be stored in accumulator A.

Programs will be written in assembly language. When a program is completed it can be hand assembled by using the programmer's card to determine op codes for the assembly statements and listing the ops. The op list can be loaded directly into the processor and run. A simple program has been assembled in Fig. 3-4. Use the programmer's card and assemble the other three.

CHAPTER 4

Accumulators

Having been exposed to assembly language and the programmer's card, the 6800 instruction set can now be examined. The set has been divided into groups of related instructions and each group will be used. The first group to be examined is the most frequently used in the 6800 set.

Objectives

You will be able to:

1. Use the LDAX and STAX instructions
2. Use the extended addressing mode
3. Write a simple data transfer program
4. Enter and run a simple data transfer program

Like instructions, data manipulated by a program is stored in memory. Arithmetic and logic operations performed on data by the processor are done in the alu. Data must be transferred into the processor before an operation can be performed on it. Two registers called accumulators are located in the 6800 to temporarily hold data moved into the processor. Data cannot be placed directly in the alu; it must first be moved into an accumulator. The accumulators are one byte wide and are referred to as accumulator A and accumulator B.

A data byte is moved from its memory location into an accumulator with the LDAX instruction. The X indicates into which accumulator the data is to be placed. LDAA indicates accumulator A, LDAB indicates accumulator B. The X suffix is used frequently with accumulator instructions allowing the programmer to choose A or B.

Notice that the LDAA operation is described on the programmer's card as M → A. Besides telling the processor to move a data byte into an accumulator with the LDAX, the program must also indicate the location of the byte in memory. Pointing the processor to the location of the desired byte is called addressing. The extended addressing mode names the location of the data explicitly by using both the high and low bytes of its address. An instruction using extended addressing requires three program bytes; the first is the op code, the second is the high byte of the data's address, the third is the low byte of the data's address. Extended addressing always indicates the complete address by listing first the high byte, then the low byte. Suppose that an operation is to be performed on data that is stored at memory location 03F9. The instruction to move the data into accumulator A is shown in Fig. 4-1.

Op	Name
B6	LDAA, extnd
03	High byte of data address
F9	Low byte of data address

Fig. 4-1. The LDAA assembled.

After an operation is performed the result must be transferred from the accumulator to memory; if it is not the next LDAX will replace it with new data and it will be lost. To move data from an accumulator to memory the STAX instruction is used. The store accumulator instruction is described as A → M or B → M and as with the LDAX the address to which the data will be moved must be provided. The extended addressing mode may be used with the STAX. Fig. 4-2 shows the STAX assembled to store the contents of accumulator B at memory location 00A2.

Occasionally you may want to duplicate the contents of a memory address or move data from one location to another. A data transfer program can be written using just the LDAX

Op	Name
F7	STAB, extnd
00	High byte of data address
A2	Low byte of data address

Fig. 4-2. The STAB assembled.

and STAX instructions. The contents of the location to be moved or duplicated are loaded into an accumulator. The contents of the accumulator are then stored at the desired new address.

Write and assemble in Fig. 4-3 a program that will move the contents of memory location 001B to location 0023. Use accumulator B and extended addressing. After you have written the data transfer program compare it with the listing of Fig. 4-4 at the end of the chapter.

Before the data transfer program, just written, can be executed by the processor it must be loaded into memory. It can be placed in any available RAM locations but for simplicity assume the address of the first instruction to be 0000.

Addresses of instructions are usually included when a program is written on a programming sheet as in Fig. 4-5. Notice that an entire instruction is contained on one line, the data address follows the op code. The Loc column lists the address of an instruction. The data address resides in the memory locations that follow the op code. Space is provided on the

Op	Name

Fig. 4-3. Write a data move program.

Loc	Code	Name
0000	F6 00 1B	LDAB, extnd
0003	F7 00 23	STAB, extnd

Fig. 4-5. The programming sheet.

sheet for the mnemonic and a comment about the instruction. Programming sheets are used because they allow programs to be easily written, assembled, and entered into the processor. They also make a program easy for other programmers to follow.

The 6800 has no provisions for directly entering the instructions and data of your data transfer program. It has just one control line that can be used to begin execution, the reset line. When the 6800 is powered up random data appears in the program counter so the processor begins executing a meaningless program. The reset line allows the programmer to gain control of the processor by forcing an address into the program counter. That address must be the location of the first instruction in a meaningful program. When the reset line is pulled low the processor will look at the highest two bytes in memory to find that address. Those bytes, FFFF and FFFE in a system with a fully expanded memory are called the reset vector. A vector is a pointer so the name is appropriate; the reset vector points to the location of the first program instruction. The reset vector is usually in nonvolatile ROM which provides a constant valid address for the reset operation. Having the reset vector in ROM works well in dedicated control systems since only one program, also in ROM, will be executed.

Developmental and hobbyist systems need the capabilities of beginning execution at various locations, entering programs and examining and changing desired memory locations. A special program called a monitor or executive provides those features for most processor systems. MIKBUG,® MINIBUG® and JBUG,® all registered by Motorola, are but three of many monitors available. A monitor resides in ROM and is pointed to by the reset vector. When the reset line is taken low the processor begins execution of the monitor program. The monitor will look for input signals from a keyboard and if it senses a signal it will perform a function. A monitor is software that allows the programmer to use hardware. You must become familiar with the monitor that resides in your system. You should know how to examine and change the contents of a memory location, begin execution of a program at a desired location, and single step through a program.

Enter the data transfer program of Fig. 4-5 beginning at 0000. After the program is in memory, go to location 001B and enter FF, the data that should be transferred to 0023 by the program. Observe and record the contents of 0023 ______. Execute the program starting the processor at 0000. Record the processor's action ______. Nothing will happen. The processor will run on and on because a stop instruction was not included in the program. Press the reset button to regain control of the processor by forcing it to execute the monitor. Use the monitor to examine 0023. Record its contents ______. You should see FF.

Rewrite and assemble in Fig. 4-6 the data transfer program so that 3E is transferred from 000F to 0011 via accumulator A.

Compare your program with the one shown in Fig. 4-7 at the end of the chapter.

Loc	Code	Name
0000		

Fig. 4-6. Write a data transfer program.

Enter and run the program. Push reset and examine 0011. If the program ran successfully 0011 should contain 3E.

Data placed in one accumulator can be moved to the other using the transfer accumulator instruction. TAB puts the contents of A in B, and TBA puts the contents of B in A. Notice on the programmer's card that the transfer accumulator instruction can be used only in inherent addressing mode. The inherent mode does not require the programmer to list an address following the instruction. Since both accumulators exist inside the 6800, it knows where they are and needs only the transfer instruction. While the extended mode requires three bytes of program memory, the inherent mode requires only one. The instruction to transfer the contents of accumulator B to accumulator A is assembled in Fig. 4-8.

Loc	Code	Name
0000	17	TBA, inher

Fig. 4-8. The assembled TBA.

Write and assemble in Fig. 4-9 a program that will transfer 3E from 0020 to accumulator A, to accumulator B, and to 0021.

Compare your program with the one shown in Fig. 4-10 at the end of the chapter.

Loc	Code	Name
0000		

Fig. 4-9. Write a data transfer program.

Enter and run your program. Reset the processor and examine the contents of 0021; 3E should be there.

These simple data transfer programs have acquainted you with the movement of data into and out of the accumulators. The LDAX and STAX will be used often.

Op	Name
F6	LDAB, extnd
00	High byte of data address
1B	Low byte of data address
F7	STAB, extnd
00	High byte of data address
23	Low byte of data address

Fig. 4-4. A data transfer program.

Loc	Code	Name
0000	B6 00 0F	LDAA, extnd
0003	B7 00 11	STAA, extnd

Fig. 4-7. Moving data through A.

Loc	Code	Name
0000	B6 00 20	LDAA, extnd
0003	16	TAB, inher
0004	F7 00 21	STAB, extnd

Fig. 4-10. Data transfer through A and B.

CHAPTER 5

Basic Program Improvements

Often after a program has been written and successfully run, a number of improvements are made. Many of these improvements are a result of the programmer's retrospective consideration of the program. Before proceeding to the next group of instructions in the 6800 set, some improvements will be made in the programs just written.

Objectives

You will be able to:

1. Single step through a program looking for errors
2. Add an end of program routine
3. Sketch the flowchart of a simple program

A program to transfer data from 24 to FA is listed in Fig. 5-1. Although this program will run, it is possible that the contents will not stay in 00FA. After executing the load and store instructions, the 6800 will attempt to execute the contents of the next location at 0006. If 0006 is executable, the processor will run wild in a random, meaningless program. During execution of this useless program, the contents of any memory location, including 00FA, may be changed. The problem

Loc	Code	Name
0000	B6 00 24	LDAA, extnd
0003	B7 00 FA	STAA, extnd
0006	?	

Fig. 5-1. A data transfer program.

could be remedied with a stop instruction at 0006. Unfortunately the 6800 instruction set does not include a stop. Instead an instruction can be placed at 0006 that will return the processor to the monitor program. That instruction is the jump which causes the processor to jump to a location that is specified and continue execution. The desired location is the first instruction in the monitor program. If your system uses the MIKBUG monitor, that location is E0E3. The entry location for the JBUG monitor is E08D. The data transfer program including the monitor return is listed in Figs. 5-2 and 5-3. Enter the appropriate program and run it.

Loc	Code	Name
0000	B6 00 24	LDAA, extnd
0003	B7 00 FA	STAA, extnd
0006	7E E0 E3	JMP, extnd, to monitor

Fig. 5-2. Data transfer with return to MIKBUG.

If your system does not use either MIKBUG or JBUG, you can determine the entry point from the program listing of the monitor. Most manufacturers supply a detailed listing of the monitor program used. Look for a location labeled start, restart, or monitor entry. When you find a possible entry location, try it in the listing of Fig. 5-2. The return to monitor is a good way to end a program and it provides a positive indication, the prompt, that the program has run.

Should the prompt not be displayed, the programmer can assume that an error exists in the program. Finding and cor-

Loc	Code	Name
0000	B6 00 24	LDAA, extnd
0003	B7 00 FA	STAA, extnd
0006	7E E0 8D	JMP, extnd, to monitor

Fig. 5-3. Data transfer with return to JBUG.

recting errors is called debugging. The first step in debugging is comparing the program entered into memory with the listing on the programming sheet and correcting any differences. If the program does not run when tried, the program listing should be examined for such errors as invalid ops or incorrect addresses. Should the program still fail to run, each instruction in the program should be examined.

Many monitors allow the programmer to observe the effects of each instruction by providing the single step function. The single step function lets the monitor direct program execution. The monitor allows one instruction to be executed and then regains control of the processor. The programmer can then examine the internal registers and determine if the instruction caused the desired effects. The programmer must signal the monitor to initiate execution of the next instruction, usually by pressing a start key. By single stepping through a program, a programmer can detect and correct errors. You should become familiar with the use of the single step function of your 6800 system. Enter the data transfer program of Fig. 5-4. Enter the proper monitor entry address and 3E at 001A.

Loc	Code	Name
0000	B6 00 1A	LDAA, extnd
0003	16	TAB
0004	F7 00 1B	STAB, extnd
0007	7E XX XX	JMP, extnd, to monitor

Fig. 5-4. A data transfer program.

Single step through the program, listing in Fig. 5-5 the observed contents of accumulator A, accumulator B, and location

Loc	ACCA	ACCB	001B
0000			
0003			
0004			
0007			

Fig. 5-5. Single stepping the data transfer program.

001B for each instruction. You should be able to see the data move into A, into B, then to 001B. Notice that each line in the listing of Fig. 5-4 represents one program step.

Change the contents of location 0003 from 16 to 1B simulating an entry error. Single step through the program as before, recording the contents of A, B, and 001B in Fig. 5-6.

Instruction at	ACCA	ACCB	Loc 001B
0000			
0003			
0004			
0007			

Fig. 5-6. Single stepping through on error.

After the execution of the instruction at 0003, the existence of an error was apparent; the TAB code was incorrectly entered. Correct the code at 0003 and run the program again to confirm its correct operation.

Enter the data transfer program listing of Fig. 5-7. Single step through the program using Fig. 5-8 and determine the error. The program should move 3E from 0020 to 0030 through 0025.

Loc	Code			Name
0000	F6	00	20	LDAB, extnd
0003	F7	00	25	STAB, extnd
0006	B6	00	25	LDAA, extnd
0009	A7	00	30	STAA, extnd
000C	7E	XX	XX	JMP, extnd, to monitor

Fig. 5-7. A questionable data transfer program.

The error is an incorrect op code for the STAA in the extended mode. Correct the error and confirm the correct operation of the program.

All of the above techniques are useful in debugging a program if the program is designed correctly. If there is a basic design error, the program will not run properly even though

Instruction at	ACCA	ACCB	0025	0030
0000				
0003				
0006				
0009				
000C				

Fig. 5-8. Single stepping Fig. 5-7.

all of the debugging techniques have been used. The programmer needs a way of examining his basic idea of how the program should accomplish the desired task. Flowcharting is a technique a programmer can use to methodically develop and debug a program.

A flowchart is a block diagram that shows how the program will accomplish its task. Flowcharting can be done on a variety

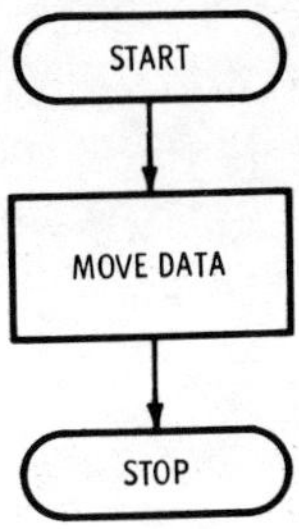

Fig. 5-9. A simple data transfer flowchart.

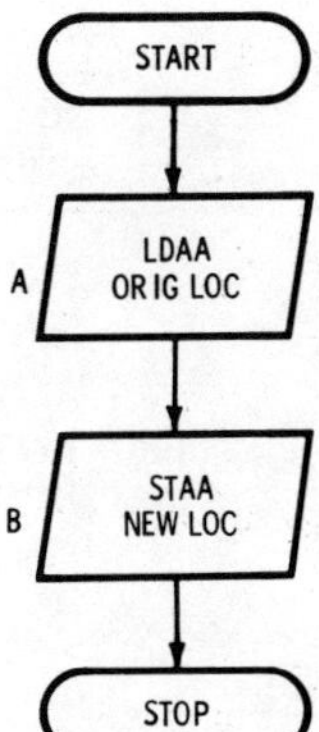

Fig. 5-10. A detailed transfer chart.

of levels. A very simple flowchart of a data transfer program is shown in Fig. 5-9. The problem is defined but no detail is listed in this flowchart. Notice the oval blocks that indicate the beginning and end of the program.

Having defined the problem in a simple flowchart, a programmer can now sketch more detailed flowcharts that represent possible solutions. The flowchart of Fig. 5-10 represents the data transfer program of Fig. 5-2. This chart includes the block shape (A and B in Fig. 5-10) used to indicate the movement of data into or out of the processor. The assembly language program could be written from this chart.

More difficult programs may require intermediate charts, each showing more detail than the last. New flowcharting symbols will be added as each group of instructions is discussed.

CHAPTER 6

Arithmetic and Logic Instructions

As the 6800 controls a process it must evaluate information it receives about the progress of the process. Evaluation includes conversion of information it receives and generation of necessary correction signals. Arithmetic and logic statements are essential elements of evaluation.

Objectives

You will be able to:

1. Write a simple addition program
2. Use the decimal correct statement
3. Write a simple subtraction program
4. Use the direct addressing mode

Addition is easily performed on the 6800. One number is loaded into an accumulator and the other is added to it using the ADDX instruction. The ADDX is described on the programmer's card as $A + M \rightarrow A$; the contents of a specified memory location are added to the contents of an accumulator and the result is stored in the accumulator. The ADDX may be used in the extended addressing mode. The flowchart of a simple addition program is shown in Fig. 6-1. The flowchart

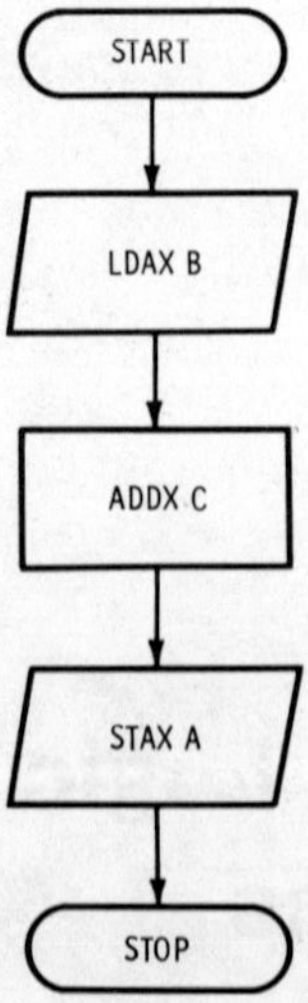

Fig. 6-1. A simple addition program.

might represent the arithmetic expression A = B + C. The ADDX appears in a rectangular block, as do all arithmetic and logic instructions. The sum, placed in the accumulator, must be stored in memory if it is to be used later.

List and assemble in Fig. 6-2 the addition program. Assume that A represents the contents of 002A, B the contents of 002B,

Loc	Code	Name
0000		

Fig. 6-2. Assemble an addition program.

and C the contents of 002C. Let B = 4 and C = 3. Compare your listing with that of Fig. 6-3 at the end of the chapter. Enter your program and run it. Examine location 002A and list its contents ______. It should contain 7, the sum of 3 and 4. The ADDX can be used repeatedly to allow a string of numbers to be added. A flowchart listing a multiple addition program is shown in Fig. 6-4. The flowchart represents the arithmetic expression A = B + C + D + E. Write and assemble this program in Fig. 6-5. Assume A, B, and C as before and that D represents the contents of 002D and E the contents of 002E. Let D = 10 and E = 6. Compare your program with the listing of Fig. 6-6 at the end of the chapter. Enter and run your program. Examine and record the contents of 002A ______. It should contain 1D, the sum of the hex numbers 10, 6, 4, and 3.

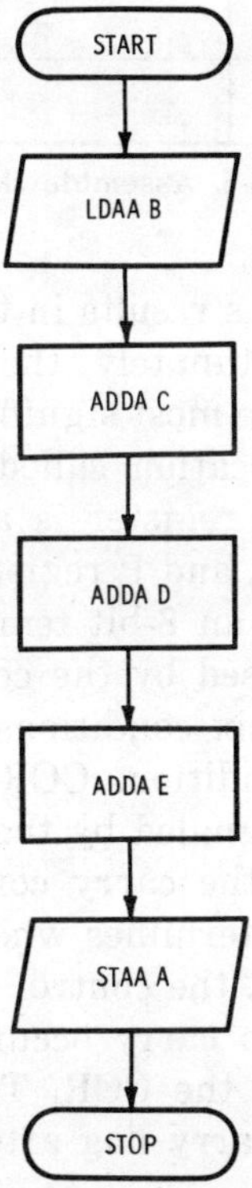

Fig. 6-4. A multiple-addition program.

Change the values of B, C, D, and E to be FE, 01, 01, and 01, respectively. Run the multiple addition program with these new values. List the number you expect to find at 002A ______. Examine 002A and list its contents ______. The sum of FE, 01, 01, and 01 is 101 but since the 6800 deals in 8-bit bytes you do not see the most significant 1. To lose that carried 1 could

Loc	Code	Name
0000		

Fig. 6-5. Assemble the multiple-addition program.

cause disastrous results in the function to be controlled by the processor. Fortunately, the 6800 has noted that a carry did occur out of the most significant bit, D7. The carry is recorded in a special location called the condition code register. The condition code register is also known as the CCR, processor status register, and P register.

The CCR is an 8-bit temporary storage location inside the 6800 that is used by the control unit to hold information on the status of six conditions. Each bit in the CCR represents a separate condition. CCR bits are often called flags since changes are signaled by their states. The least significant bit, D0, indicates the carry condition. After each operation, the control unit determines whether a carry was generated. When a carry occurs, the control unit sets, puts a one, in D0 of the CCR. When no carry occurs, the control unit resets, puts a zero, in D0 of the CCR. The control unit automatically sets or resets the carry flag after every operation that could generate a carry.

By examining the CCR after addition, a carry becomes immediately apparent. The right-hand column of the programmer's card indicates those flags affected by each operation. The H, I, N, Z, and V flags will be discussed with appropriate instructions. Notice that the ADDX does affect the carry flag. If a carry is generated by ADDX, the carry flag will be set. If a carry exists from a previous addition, the ADDX will not include the carry and the resulting sum will be less than it should be. Then the ADDX must not be used when the need to include a possible carry exists.

Run the multiple addition program of Fig. 6-6 in the single step mode and record in Fig. 6-7 the contents of the accumulator and the CCR after each step. Since the carry flag is D0, the CCR will contain an even number when the carry is reset and an odd number when the carry is set. The carry flag's

Loc	ACCA	CCR
0000		
0003		
0006		
0009		
000C		

Fig. 6-7. Observing the carry flag.

initial condition is unpredictable since it assumes a random condition when the processor is powered up. The LDAA has no effect on the flag as seen on the programmer's card. Each ADDA affects the flag. It is reset after 0003, set after 0006, and reset after 0009. The carry can be detected and allowed for in the program.

The carry did not affect the sum since the ADDA ignores the carry. If it is desirable to include an existing carry in the addition, another instruction, the ADCX, must be used. The ADCX is represented as A + M + C → A on the programmer's card. Substitute B9, the ADCA op code, for the ADDA at locations 0003, 0006, and 0009 in the multiple addition program of Fig. 6-6. Execute the program in the single step mode recording in Fig. 6-8 the contents of the accumulator and CCR after each step. When the carry was set, after 0006, the carry was included in the sum; when it was reset, the carry zero was included in the sum.

Since the carry flag can initially be either set or reset, the programmer must be able to control its condition. The clear carry instruction can be used to reset the carry flag before the

Loc	ACCA	CCR
0000		
0003		
0006		
0009		
000C		

Fig. 6-8. Observing the carry and the ADCX.

first ADCX in a program. Only the carry flag is affected by the CLC; the other CCR flags remain unchanged. Listed on the programmer's card as OC and CLC, clear carry is used only in the inherent addressing mode and requires only one byte of program storage. Write and assemble in Fig. 6-10 the addition program flowcharted in Fig. 6-9. Assume A, B, and C as before and let B = 4A and C = A5. Compare your listing

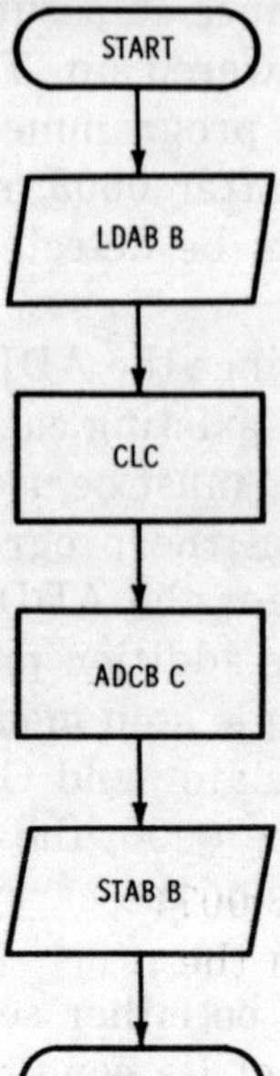

Fig. 6-9. Addition including the carry.

with that of Fig. 6-11 at the end of the chapter. Enter and run the program. Examine and record the contents of A ______.

Loc	Code	Name
0000		

Fig. 6-10. Assembling a carry program.

Being an 8-bit machine, the 6800 can directly handle numbers as large as 255. A larger number can be handled by allowing it to occupy more than one memory byte. A two-byte number can be as large as 65,535, a three-byte number as large as 16,777,215. A multiple-byte number is usually assigned adjacent memory locations. Arithmetic functions are performed first on the least significant byte, then on the more significant bytes. Carries generated by addition of the least significant bytes are included in the more significant byte additions. Addition of two two-byte numbers is shown in Fig. 6-12. Another two-byte method using both accumulators is shown in Fig. 6-13.

Write and assemble in Fig. 6-14 the two-byte addition program of Fig. 6-13. Assume that number 1 is at 0050 and 0051 and that number 2 is at 0060 and 0061. Let the lower address of each number be its most significant byte. Let number 1 = 0623 and number 2 = 0149. Store the sum at 0070 and 0071. Compare your listing with that of Fig. 6-15 at the end of the chapter. Enter and run your program. Examine and list the contents of location 0070 and 0071 ______________. The sum of 0623 and 0149 is 076C. Run the program again letting number 1 = 01FF and number 2 = 0601. The sum, 0800, was obtained with the addition of the carry from the least significant sum.

The addition program just written can be greatly shortened by replacing the extended addressing mode with the direct mode. An instruction used in the direct mode can access any of the first 256 bytes. It can also be used to advantage in longer programs if variable data locations are assigned page zero addresses.

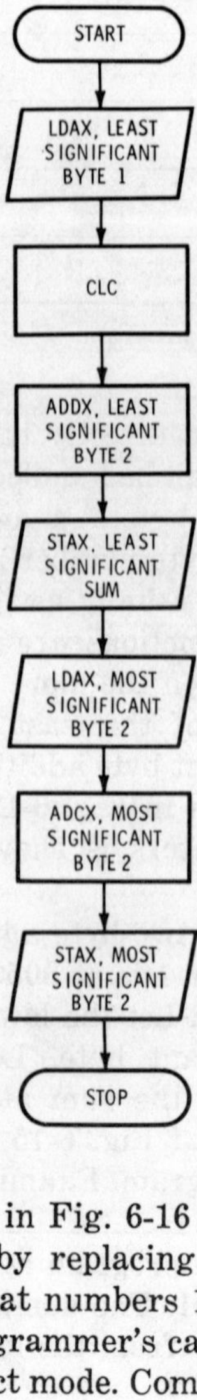

Fig. 6-12. Multiple-byte addition.

Rewrite in Fig. 6-16 the multiple byte addition program of Fig. 6-15 by replacing the extended with direct addressing. Assume that numbers 1, 2 and the sum are the same. Notice on the programmer's card that not all instructions can be used in the direct mode. Compare your listing with that of Fig. 6-17

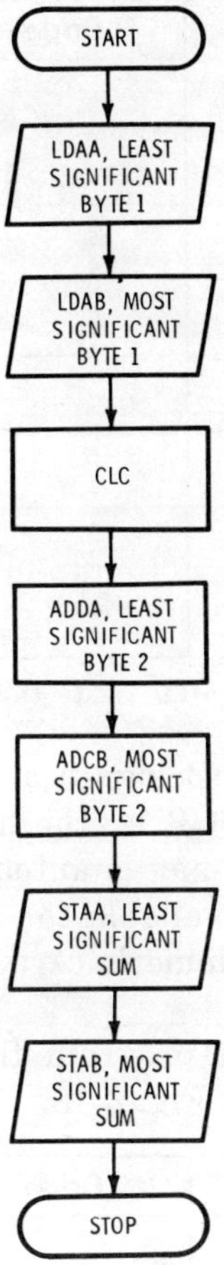

Fig. 6-13. Two-byte addition.

at the end of the chapter. Enter and run the program. The sum 800 should not change.

In consumer applications the 6800 must present its data to the operator in decimal form. A grocery cashier could have problems making change for a $1110 0111 or $E7 total. The 6800 can perform decimal addition using the ADDX, ADCX, or ABA and the decimal adjust instruction. Since the 6800 uses 8-bit data words, the contents of each byte are interpreted as two binary coded decimal characters when the DAA is used. The BCD code represents any of the unique decimal digits in 4-bit binary. The DAA also adjusts the carry flag to indicate a decimal number greater than 99. A carry from the least signifi-

Loc	Code	Name
0000		

Fig. 6-14. Write the multibyte-addition program.

cant to the most significant BCD character of a byte is indicated in the CCR by the half carry flag. Like the carry flag, the half carry flag is automatically set and reset by the processor and is available for use by the programmer. As shown on the programmer's card, the H flag is bit position 5 in the CCR.

An addition program that includes the decimal adjust is flowcharted in Fig. 6-18.

Loc	Code	Name
0000		

Fig. 6-16. Writing an addition program using direct addressing.

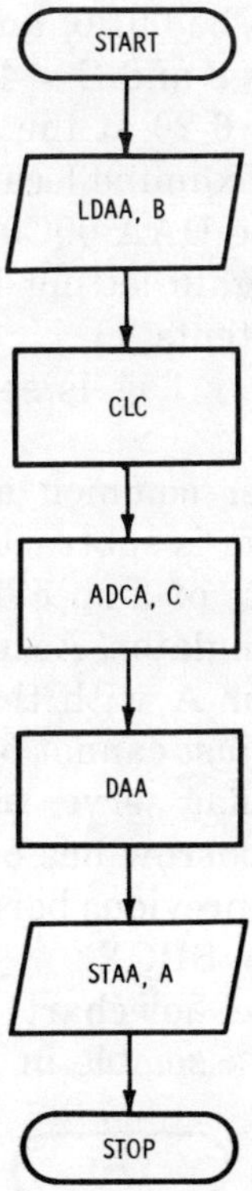

Fig. 6-18. A decimal-addition program.

Write and assemble the program in Fig. 6-19. Notice that the DAA can be used only in the inherent mode and requires only one byte of program memory. Assume A to be location

Loc	Code	Name
0000		

Fig. 6-19. Writing the decimal-addition program.

00A0, B to be 00B0, and C to be 00C0. Use direct addressing and let B = 8 and C = 4. Compare your program with the listing of Fig. 6-20 at the end of the chapter. Enter and run the program. Examine location 00C0 and list its contents ______. Without the DAA 00C0 would contain the hex sum C. Run the program again letting B = 45 and C = 70. Examine 00C0 and list its contents ______. Examine the CCR and determine if the carry flag is set or reset. Carry flag C should be set.

The other common arithmetic function that the processor can perform is subtraction. The subtract instruction subtracts the contents of a specified memory location from the contents of an accumulator. Accumulator B can also be subtracted from accumulator A with the SBA instruction. Unfortunately, the decimal adjust cannot be used with the subtraction instruction. The carry flag serves as the borrow flag in subtraction, when it is set a borrow has occurred. Subtraction can be performed ignoring a previous borrow, the SUBX, or including a previous borrow, the SBCX.

A simple flowchart of A = B − C is shown in Fig. 6-21. Write and assemble in Fig. 6-22 the program using direct ad-

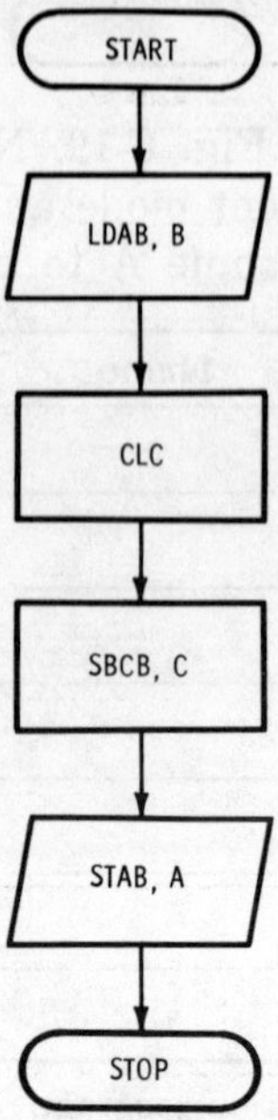

Fig. 6-21. A simple subtraction program.

Loc	Code	Name
0000		

Fig. 6-22. Writing the subtraction program.

dressing. Assume A to be location 00A0, B to be 00B0, and C to be 00C0. Let B = 6 and C = 4. Just as in addition, the carry flag must be reset. Compare your program with the listing of Fig. 6-23 at the end of the chapter. Enter and run the program. Examine 00A0 and list its contents ______. Set the carry flag by examining the CCR and altering its contents to an odd number. Run the program again. The difference at 00A0 should be 1 since a borrow was also subtracted.

Loc	Code	Name

Fig. 6-25. Writing a multibyte-subtraction program.

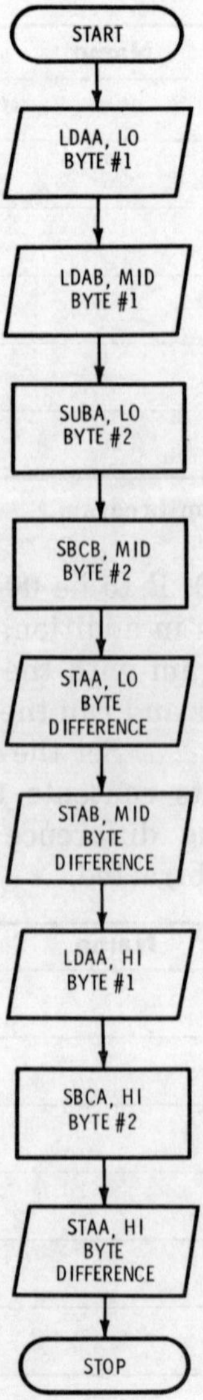

Fig. 6-24. Multibyte subtraction.

Multiple-byte subtraction can be performed and is similar to multiple-byte addition. The flowchart of Fig. 6-24 shows the subtraction of two three-byte numbers.

As in addition, the least significant bytes are subtracted first followed by the subtraction of the most significant bytes with the borrow flag linking the operations. Write and assemble the multibyte subtraction in Fig. 6-25. Assume number 1 is located at 00A0, A1, and A2 with the most significant byte residing at A0. Also assume number 2 is located at 00B0, B1, and B2. Put the difference at 00C0, C1, and C2.

Compare your program with the listing of Fig. 6-26 at the end of the chapter. Enter your program, letting number 1 = A26350 and number 2 = 134020. Run the program. Examine and list the difference ______. Change number 2 to 134074 and run the program again. Examine and list the difference ______. The difference is not as expected because the processor handles numbers that are smaller than zero, negatives, in their two's complement form.

Loc	Code	Name
0000	B6 00 2B	LDAA, extnd, B
0003	BB 00 2C	ADDA, extnd, C
0006	B7 00 2A	STAA, extnd, A
0009	7E XX XX	JMP, extnd, monitor

Fig. 6-3. The assembled-addition program.

Loc	Code	Name
0000	B6 00 2B	LDAA, extnd, B
0003	BB 00 2C	ADDA, extnd, C
0006	BB 00 2D	ADDA, extnd, D
0009	BB 00 2E	ADDA, extnd, E
000C	B7 00 2A	STAA, extnd, A
000F	7E XX XX	JMP, extnd, monitor

Fig. 6-6. The assembled multiple-addition program.

Loc	Code	Name
0000	F6 00 2B	LDAB, extnd, B
0003	0C	CLC
0004	F9 00 2C	ADCB, extnd, C
0007	F7 00 2A	STAB, extnd, A
000A	7E XX XX	JMP, extnd, monitor

Fig. 6-11. The assembled-carry program.

Loc	Code	Name
0000	B6 00 51	LDAA, extnd, LS Byte 1
0003	F6 00 50	LDAB, extnd, MS Byte 1
0006	BB 00 61	ADDA, extnd, LS Byte 2
0009	F9 00 60	ADCB, extnd, MS Byte 2
000C	B7 00 71	STAA, extnd, LS Sum
000F	F7 00 70	STAB, extnd, MS Sum
0012	7E XX XX	JMP, extnd, monitor

Fig. 6-15. The multibyte-addition program assembled.

Loc	Code	Name
0000	96 51	LDAA, direct, LS Byte 1
0002	D6 50	LDAB, direct, MS Byte 1
0004	9B 61	ADDA, direct, LS Byte 2
0006	D9 60	ADCB, direct, MS Byte 2
0008	97 71	STAA, LS Sum
000A	D7 70	STAB, MS Sum
000C	7E XX XX	JMP, extnd, monitor

Fig. 6-17. The assembled direct-addition program.

Loc	Code	Name
0000	96 B0	LDAA, direct, B
0002	0C	CLC
0003	99 C0	ADCA, direct, C
0005	19	DAA
0006	97 A0	STAA, A
0008	7E XX XX	JMP, extnd, monitor

Fig. 6-20. The assembled decimal-addition program.

Loc	Code	Name
0000	D6 B0	LDAB, direct, B
0002	0C	CLC
0003	D2 C0	SBCB, direct, C
0005	D7 A0	STAB, direct, A
0007	7E XX XX	JMP, extnd, monitor

Fig. 6-23. The assembled subtraction program.

Loc	Code	Name
0000	96 A2	LDAA, direct, Lo #1
0002	D6 A1	LDAB, direct, Mid #1
0004	90 B2	SUBA, direct, Lo #2
0006	D2 B1	SBCB, direct, Mid #2
0008	97 C2	STAA, direct, Lo diff
000A	D7 C1	STAB, direct, Mid diff
000C	96 A0	LDAA, direct, Hi #1
000E	92 B0	SBCA, direct, Hi #2
0010	97 C0	STAA, direct, Hi diff
0012	7E XX XX	JMP, extnd, monitor

Fig. 6-26. The assembled multibyte-subtraction program.

CHAPTER 7

More Arithmetic and Logic Instructions

Although addition and subtraction are widely used, the 6800 has other arithmetic and a wide variety of logic instructions available to the programmer. Before examining those, the treatment of negative numbers by the 6800 should be examined.

Objectives

You will be able to:

1. Convert a binary number to AND from its two's complement form
2. Use the negative AND overflow flags
3. Use the 6800's logic instructions
4. Use the immediate addressing mode

Enter the subtraction program of Fig. 7-1. Assume A to be at 00A0, B at 00B0, and C at 00C0. Let B = 6 and C = 4.

Run the program and examine A to verify that the program is correct. Run the program again letting B = 4 and C = 6. Examine and list the contents of A ______. The expected answer, −2, is at 00A0 in its two's complement form, FE. The 6800 deals with negative numbers only in two's complement. To con-

Loc	Code	Name
0000	D6 BP	LDAB, direct, B
0002	0C	CLC
0003	D2 C0	SBCB, direct, C
0005	D7 A0	STAB, direct, A
0007	7E XX XX	JMP, extnd, monitor

Fig. 7-1. A simple subtraction program.

vert a number into two's complement from the one's complement, first change all the ones to zeros and zeros to ones, as in Fig. 7-2. One is then added to the one's complement to obtain the two's complement. Find the two's complement of each of the numbers in Fig. 7-3.

```
04 is  0000 0100   binary
       1111 1011   1's complement
       +        1
       ---------
       1111 1100   2's complement
          F    C   2's complement

6D is  0110 1101   binary
       1001 0010   1's complement
       +        1
       ---------
       1001 0011   2's complement
            9 3    2's complement
```

Fig. 7-2. Finding the two's complement of a number.

Any negative number involved in addition or subtraction must be in its two's complement form. Fortunately the 6800 has an instruction, the negate, that will find the two's complement of a number in either accumulator, NEGX, or a memory location, NEG. A program that will calculate the two's complement of each of two numbers is flowcharted in Fig. 7-4.

Write and assemble the program in Fig. 7-5. Let A = 13 at location 00A0. Store the contents of B at location 00B0. Let C = D5 at 00C0. Compare your program with the listing of Fig. 7-6 at the end of the chapter.

Enter and run your program. The values of B and C, ED and 2B, should be the values hand calculated in Fig. 7-3. NEG at 0005 replaced the contents of C0 with its two's complement

13 is
D5 is

Fig. 7-3. Finding the two's complements.

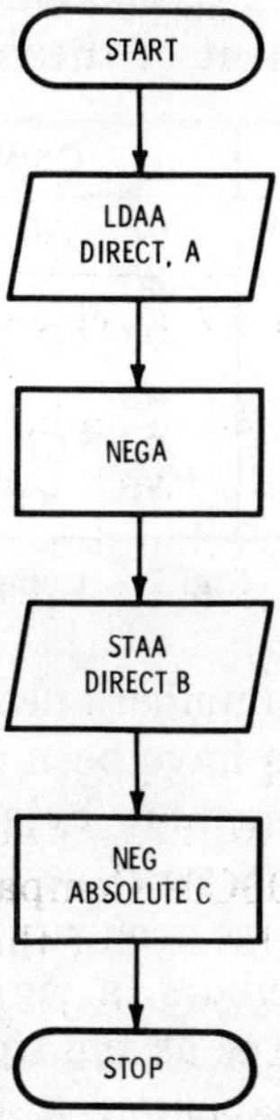

Fig. 7-4. Using the negate instruction.

Loc	Code	Name
0000		

Fig. 7-5. Writing the two's complement program.

but in the process wiped out the original contents. If the original contents are needed later in the program, they can be duplicated in another location before the NEG or the number can be loaded into an accumulator, as A was, and the NEGX used.

The listing of Fig. 7-7 is a program that finds the two's complement of a two's complement. Enter the program, letting A = 13 at 00A0. Run the program. Examine 00B0 and list its contents ______. Examine 00C0 and list its contents ______. The complement of the complement is the original number.

Loc	Code	Name
0000	96 A0	LDAA, direct, A
0002	40	NEGA
0003	97 B0	STAA, direct, B
0005	40	NEGA
0006	97 C0	STAA, direct, C
0008	7E XX XX	JMP, extnd, monitor

Fig. 7-7. Complementing the complement.

All of the numbers dealt with thus far have been unsigned, no provisions have been made to detect negative numbers. By looking at a memory byte it is impossible to determine whether FE represents positive FE or negative two in two's complement. When a program might encounter either positive or negative numbers, a sign bit must be included in each data byte. D7 serves as the sign bit. If it is set the byte contains a negative number; if it is reset the byte contains a positive number. Since D7 is used as the sign bit, each byte has just seven data bits, allowing it a maximum of 127 decimal, 7F hex. The processor notes the sign of the byte being used with a bit in the CCR, the N flag. The negative flag, bit 3 in the CCR, is automatically set and reset by the control unit and is affected by most accumulator and memory operations. If the most significant bit, D7, of the data byte being used is set, the negative flag is also set; if D7 is reset, the negative flag is also reset. By examining the negative flag the contents of a byte can be properly interpreted.

When the sign bit is used, the carry flag is meaningless since it represents a carry out of D7, now the sign bit. A special bit in the CCR, the V flag, indicates a carry out of D6 and is used with signed numbers. The overflow flag occupies bit 1 in the CCR and, like the carry flag, is automatically set and reset by the control unit to reflect a carry out of D6. When the overflow flag is set by an operation the sign bit must be observed for a possible, erroneous change. If −103 is added to −64 an overflow carry is generated, the V flag is set and the overflow carry from D6 is added to D7, the sign bit. Since the numbers are negative the sign bit is initially set and, when the overflow

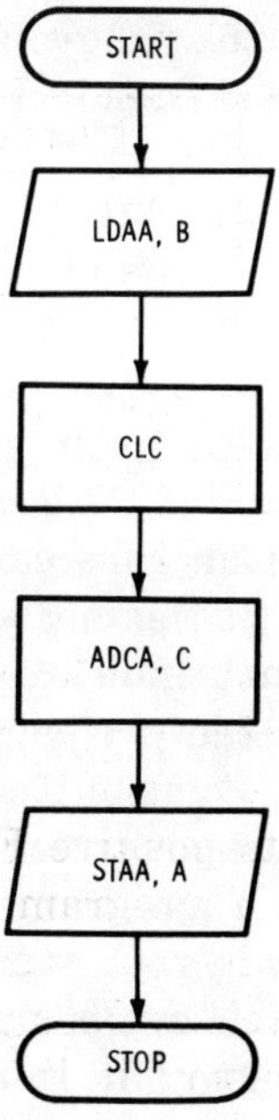

Fig. 7-8. A simple addition program.

Loc	CCR	N flag	V flag	C flag
0000				
0002				
0003				
0005				
0007				

Fig. 7-10. Observing the overflow.

carry is added, it becomes zero. The sum of −103 and −64 is not positive as the sign bit would indicate, so both the sign and overflow flags must be observed. The flowchart of Fig. 7-8 shows a simple addition program. The program has been written and assembled in Fig. 7-9. Enter the program and assume A to be the contents of 00A0, B the contents of 00B0, and C the contents of 00C0. Let B = +70 and C = +30. The use of signed numbers limits the value of a byte to 7F. One more than 7F, 80, is not allowed since it involves D7, the sign bit. Single step through the program and record the CCR's contents and the N, V, and C flags in Fig. 7-10. After 0000 the negative flag is reset indicating that a positive number has been loaded into the accumulator. After 0003 the overflow flag signals a carry out of D6 which is added to and sets the negative flag. In fact, the sum is not negative and should be changed to reflect the positive sum with a carry, a process covered in Chapter 8.

Look at the program again. If the numbers are assumed to be unsigned and if D7 is considered a data bit instead of a sign bit, the program runs correctly. In hex 70 plus 30 equals A0. The flowchart assembly and machine code listings of Figs. 7-8 and 7-9 do not indicate, in any way, that the data used is signed. Only the programmer's interpretation of the sum at C and the CCR make it signed. It is important to understand that the programmer defines the data. He can choose to ignore the N and V flags and work quite well with 8-bit unsigned numbers, always providing negatives in two's complement. Many programs can be written more efficiently using unsigned numbers and most in this text will be in that form. However, some arithmetic programs depend on the use of the N and V flags to indicate the proper interpretation of signed data. In developing a program the technique that best suits the nature of data encountered should be used.

Two other arithmetic instructions are available for use with the 6800. The ASL (arithmetic shift left) instruction moves the contents of each bit in a byte left one position, like musical chairs. The contents of D0 move to D1; the contents of D1 move to D2, etc. The contents of D7, the most significant bit, are moved to the carry flag in the CCR and the least significant bit D0 is always given a zero. The ASL, as shown in Fig. 7-11 and on the programmer's card, can be used with either accumulator or a memory location. A simple shift program is flowcharted in Fig. 7-12. Write and assemble the program in Fig. 7-13. A is 00A0 and equals AA. Compare your listing with that of Fig. 7-14 at the end of the chapter.

Enter and run the program; list A ______. Run the program again without modifying A; list A ______. Run the program six more times examining A after each run. You should

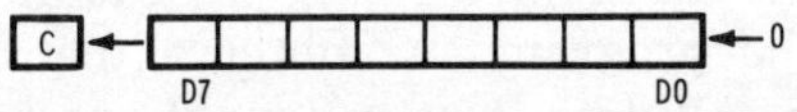

Fig. 7-11. The ASL instructions move the contents of each bit in a byte left one position.

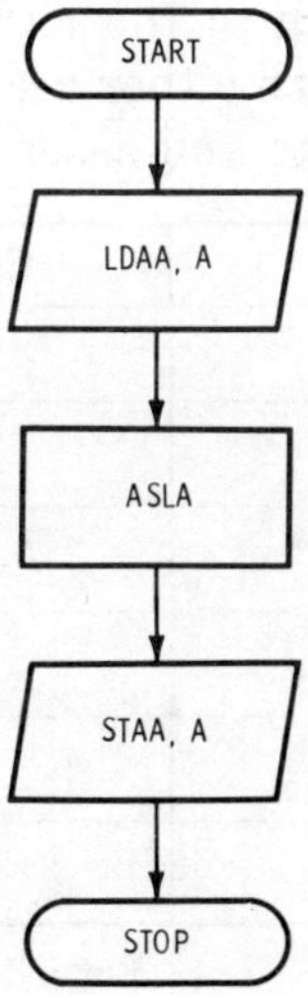

Fig. 7-12. A simple shift program.

Loc	Code	Name
0000		

Fig. 7-13. Writing the shift program.

be able to see the number moving left. After any data is shifted from D7 into the carry, the next shift causes it to fall out of the carry bit into space. It is then gone, forever lost. If a number is to be used in its original form after a multiple shift, it must be either duplicated in another memory location or loaded into an accumulator and shifted, leaving the original data intact.

Change the ASLA in 0002 of Fig. 7-14 to an ASRA, 47. Let A = 80. Run the program and observe the arithmetic shift right operation. All data is moved right one bit position with the data in D7 being repeated there. Data in D0 is shifted into the carry bit of the CCR. Data shifted out of the carry bit is forever lost. Run the program 7 more times and watch the ones march to the right. As with the ASLX, the ASRX can be used with either accumulator, ASRX, or a memory location, ASR. Write and assemble in Fig. 7-15 a simple program that

Loc	Code	Name
0000		

Fig. 7-15. Writing a shift program.

will shift data in 00A0 without transferring it to an accumulator. The program needs only two steps, the shift instruction and the stop routine.

Compare your program with the following listing: 77 00 AO 7E XX XX. Enter and run the program; assume A is 80. If the program is run again the data becomes E0. Notice, however, that the original data in 00A0 is lost. Both arithmetic shifts find wide use in math routines.

Two logic expressions that are similar to the arithmetic shifts are the rotate instructions. The rotate left moves each bit of a byte left one position. D7 is moved into the carry bit as in the arithmetic shift but the rotate uses a wrap around action that moves the carry into D0 as shown in Fig. 7-16. The

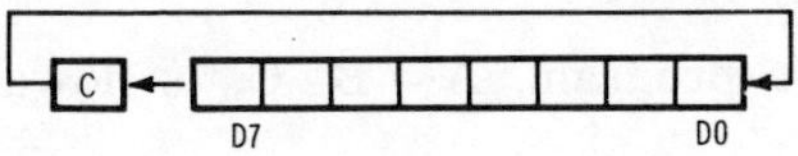

Fig. 7-16. The wrap around action moves the carry into D_0.

rotate left is on the programmer's card. Data is not lost in a rotate operation, it is only moved. The rotate right performs the same operation but each bit is shifted to the right with D0 being moved into the carry bit and the carry moved into D7. Both rotate instructions may be used with either accumulator or a memory location.

Assemble the simple rotate program as listed in Fig. 7-17. This program rotates left the data of A in accumulator A and rotates right the data in B. Assume A is 3E at 00A0 and B is 3E at 00B0. Enter and run the program nine times, observing the data at A and B after each run. The data should be in its original form after the ninth run. If it is not, the monitor may be affecting the CCR, including the carry flag, when it regains control at the end of each run. A combination of the

Loc	Code	Name
0000		LDAA, direct, A
0002		ROLA
0003		STAA, direct, A
0005		ROR, extnd, B
0008		JMP, extnd, monitor

Fig. 7-17. Assemble the rotate program.

shift and rotate operations is available in the logic shift right instruction. The LSR moves data one bit right always moving a zero into D7, moving D0 into the carry and moving the carry contents out into oblivion. It can be used with an accumulator or a memory location. Like the shifts, the rotate instructions are useful in performing math functions. They will be used to develop a multiplication routine in Chapter 9.

The 6800 is capable of performing the basic logic functions; AND, OR, EXCLUSIVE OR, and INVERT. AND, OR, and EOR perform their operations on a byte in memory and a byte in the accumulator. The operations are performed on a bit to bit basis, D0 in the accumulator is used in the operation with D0 in the specified memory location. D1 in the accumulator is used with D1 in memory, etc. The results of the operations are placed in an accumulator.

A simple AND program, A = B · C, is flowcharted in Fig. 7-18.

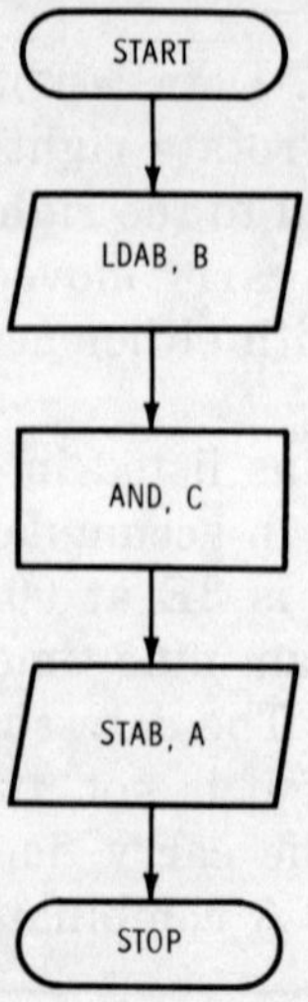

Fig. 7-18. A simple AND program.

Write and assemble the program in Fig. 7-19. Assume B is 1010 1010 at location 00B0 and C is 1100 1100 at location 00C0. Compare your program with the listing of Fig. 7-20 at the end of the chapter. Enter and run your program. Examine A and list its contents in binary ______. Notice that the AND yields a one only when both bits in the operation are one.

Loc	Code	Name
0000		

Fig. 7-19. Writing the AND program.

Substitute DA, the ORB op, for the AND op at 0002 and run the program again. Examine A and list its contents in binary ______. The ORB yields a one if either or both bits involved are one. Substitute D8, the EORB op, for the ORB op at 0002 and run the program again. Examine A and list its contents in binary ______. The EORB yields a one when either, but not both, bits are one. Substitute 53, the COMB op, for the EORB op at 0002, move the other bytes up and run the program again. Examine A and list its contents in binary ______. The COMX instruction simply inverts the data in the accumulator. By following an AND or OR instruction with a complement instruction the NAND or NOR function can be performed.

A typical use of the arithmetic logic group is sign correction during signed arithmetic. The sign bit, D-7, can be incorrectly changed by an overflow carry or borrow from D6. The processor would add +110 to +42 and produce a sum of −24 with an overflow carry. In binary 0110 1110 + 0010 1010 = 1001 1000. Only D7, the sign, should be changed; D0 – D6 are correct. Adding 1000 0000 to the sum will change the sign bit and leave D0 – D6 unchanged. This solution will work when the

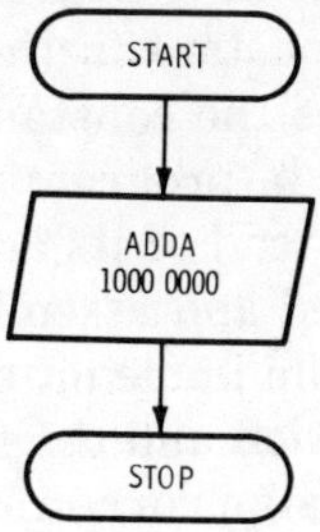

Fig. 7-21. A simple sign routine.

Loc	Code	Name
0000	8B 80	ADDA, immed, 1000 0000

Fig. 7-22. The correction program using immediate addressing.

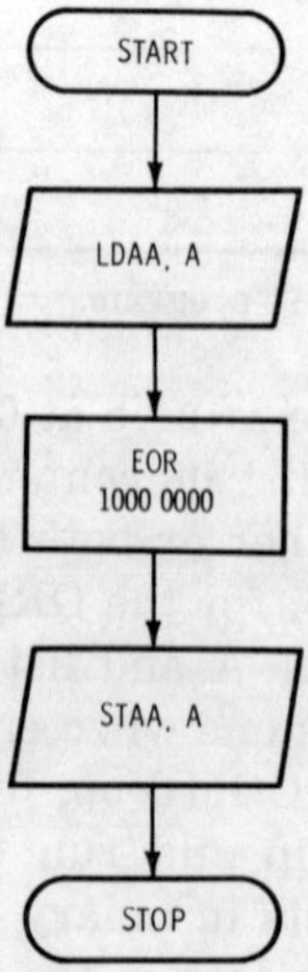

Fig. 7-23. An EOR sign correction program.

sign should be either positive or negative. A flowchart of this simple solution is shown in Fig. 7-21. The original sum is assumed to be in accumulator A after the sign changing operation and the corrected sum is not stored in memory. For any number in the accumulator one must be added to D7 to correct the sign.

Many programs contain numbers that, like 1000 0000, remain constant for any set of variables. The 6800 is equipped with an addressing mode that simplifies the use of constants. Called immediate addressing, it allows the programmer to include the constant in the program listing. Immediate addressing requires the constant data used immediately to follow the instruction in program memory. Unlike other modes, the data is listed instead of its address. The correction program of Fig. 7-21 is listed and assembled in Fig. 7-22. When an instruction is used in the immediate mode two bytes are required, one for the instruction and the following one for the constant data.

Another sign correction program is flowcharted in Fig. 7-23.

The EOR instruction performs the required correction when 80 is used. Write and assemble the program in Fig. 7-24. Assume A is E2 at 00A0 and use the EOR in the immediate mode.

Compare your listing with that of Fig. 7-25 at the end of the chapter. Enter and run the program to verify its proper operation.

Loc	Code	Name
0000		

Fig. 7-24. Writing the EOR sign correction program.

This program will make the required correction but one important element is missing. Neither the flowchart of Fig. 7-21 nor the program of Fig. 7-23 has provisions to detect the overflow carry and resulting sign change. A group of instructions that can make this determination are discussed in Chapter 8.

Loc	Code	Name
0000	96 A0	LDAA, direct, A
0002	40	NEGA
0003	97 B0	STAA, direct, B
0005	70 00 C0	NEG, extnd, C
0008	7E XX XX	JMP, extnd, monitor

Fig. 7-6. The assembled two's complement program.

Loc	Code	Name
0000	96 B0	LDAA, direct, B
0002	0C	CLC
0003	99 C0	ADCA, direct, C
0005	97 A0	STAA, direct, A
0007	7E XX XX	JMP, extnd, monitor

Fig. 7-9. The assembled addition program.

Loc	Code	Name
0000	96 A0	LDAA, direct, A
0002	48	ASLA
0003	97 A0	STAA, direct, A
0005	7E XX XX	JMP, extnd, monitor

Fig. 7-14. The assembled shift program.

Loc	Code	Name
0000	D6 B0	LDAB, direct, B
0002	D4 C0	ANDB, direct, C
0004	D7 A0	STAB, direct, A
0006	7E XX XX	JMP, extnd, monitor

Fig. 7-20. The assembled AND program.

Loc	Code	Name
0000	96 A0	LDAA, direct, A
0002	88 80	EOR, immed, 80
0004	97 A0	STAA, direct, A
0006	7E XX XX	JMP, extnd, monitor

Fig. 7-25. The assembled sign correction program.

CHAPTER 8

Branch Instructions

The CCR contains flags that will indicate important changes in the processor during program execution. A program is much more efficient if it can examine the flags and determine when corrections need to be made. The branch instructions allow the processor to evaluate the flags and make decisions based on its observations.

Objectives

You will be able to:

1. Use the branch instructions
2. Use relative addressing
3. Write an offset calculation program
4. Use the JMP instruction

The sign correction program developed in Chapter 7 can only be used effectively if the processor can detect an erroneous sign change. The program should correct the sign when needed and do nothing when the sign is correct. The branch instructions allow the processor to choose one of the two courses of action based on the condition of a selected flag. When, in signed arithmetic, a carry or borrow occurs out of D6 the sign bit is incorrectly changed and the V flag is set. The Branch on Overflow Set, BVS, or Branch on Overflow Clear, BVC, can be

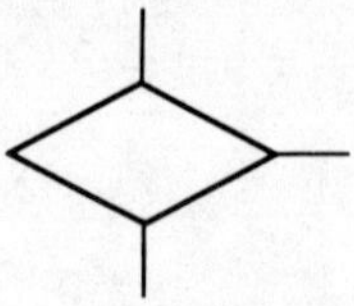

Fig. 8-1. Flowchart symbol for all branch instructions.

used to detect an incorrect sign change. The BVC does not take the branch, does nothing, when the V flag is set and the instruction that follows it is executed as usual. If the V flag is reset, the branch is taken and the contents of the program counter are replaced with an address specified by the BVC. Since the program counter always contains the address of the next instruction to be executed, the branch effectively transfers control to another section of the program and execution continues. The condition of the flag specified determines whether or not the branch will be taken. The flowchart symbol for all of the branch instructions is shown in Fig. 8-1, and the condition tested is listed inside the symbol. An addition program that includes sign correction is flowcharted in Fig. 8-2.

After the addition is performed in Fig. 8-2, the BVC examines the V flag in the CCR. If it is set indicating an incorrect sign change, the next instruction in the program is executed that corrects the sign. If the V flag is clear, the address of the STAA is jammed into the PC replacing the address of the EORA and the correction instruction is skipped. In either case, the STAA is executed normally.

Branch instructions require two bytes of program memory. The first byte is the instruction's op code. The second byte specifies the destination address if the branch is taken. Notice on the programmer's card that the branch instructions can be used only in the relative addressing mode.

The relative addressing mode specifies an address based on the current contents of the PC and a number called the offset that is listed immediately after the branch instruction. The sum of the PC and the offset becomes the destination address that is jammed into the PC when the branch is taken. The offset is the second byte of a branch instruction that limits the move to maximums of +127 or −128 bytes. Because it always points to the next instruction, the PC contains the address of the branch instruction plus two. An offset can be calculated using this formula:

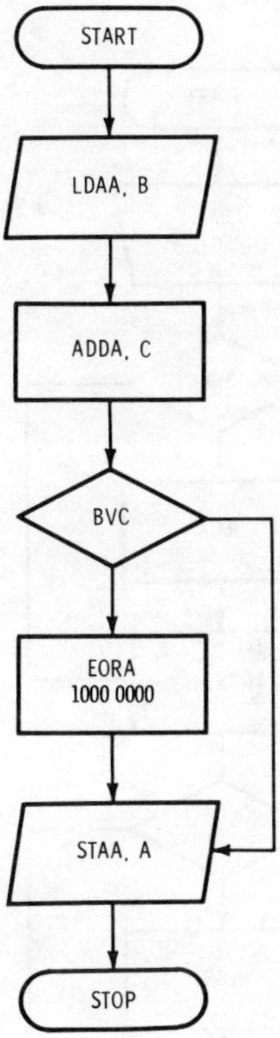

Fig. 8-2. An automatic sign correction using the BVC.

Offset = Destination address – PC.

The program of Fig. 8-2 is written and assembled in Fig. 8-3. Calculate the offset required to cause the program to skip to the STAA at 0008 if the V is clear. Remember the PC always points to the next instruction ______. Using the above formula, the offset is 0008 – 0006 = 02. Ordinarily, an offset is calculated after the program has been written and the destination address is known. Enter the program assuming B to be 32 at 00B0 and C to be 0018 at 00C0. Single step through the program and list the contents of A ______. Since the sum, 4A, did not cause an overflow carry, the branch was taken and the EORA skipped. Change C to 5E and single step through the program again. Examine A and list its contents ______.

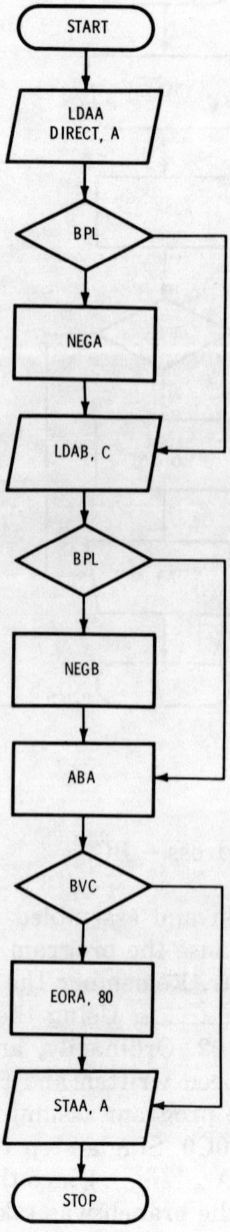

Fig. 8-4. The addition program.

The branch was not taken since the V flag was set by the addition of 32 and 5E. The sign was corrected and the sum stored.

The addition program would be more convenient if the processor could detect and convert negatives into two's complement form. It can if the Branch if Plus BPL, instruction is used as shown in Fig. 8-4.

The BPL in Fig. 8-4 determines if the number is negative; if it is, the conversion is performed, if it is not, the branch is taken. B is converted in accumulator A, and C is converted in accumulator B. The ABA adds the contents of the accumulators. The programmer indicates a negative by making the sign bit, D7, one. Write and assemble the program of Fig. 8-4 in Fig. 8-5. Assume B is +14 at 00B0 and C is +10 at 00C0.

Loc	Code	Name
0000		

Fig. 8-5. Writing the addition program.

Compare your listing with that of Fig. 8-6 at the end of the chapter. Enter and run the program. Examine A and record its contents ________. Since B and C are positive, the sum should be 24. Change B to −5 and C to +7 and run the program again. B must be entered as 85, indicating a negative 5. Examine A and list its contents ______. Change B to −4 and C to −3, run the program again. Examine A and list its contents ______. The sum, −7, is in its two's complement form.

Many process control applications use the concepts in the program just developed. Data gathered about the process is compared with ideal data stored in memory. A correction signal based on the comparison will be formulated by the program. In such a comparison three conditions are possible: the real data will be lower, the same, or higher than the ideal data. The processor must be directed to the appropriate correction routine in the program. A simple flowchart of such a decision making process is shown in Fig. 8-7.

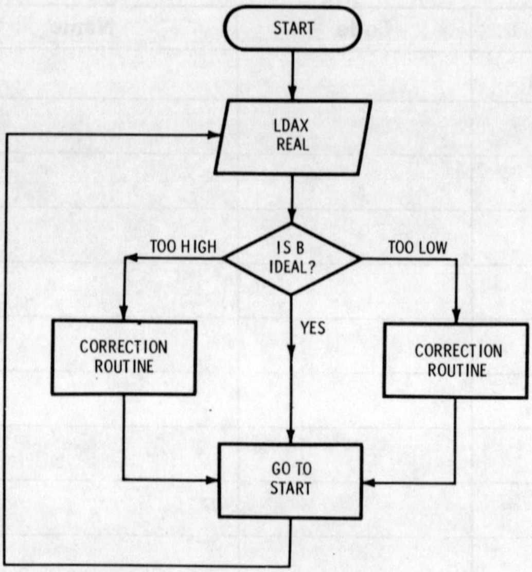

Fig. 8-7. Controlling a process.

Although the data is compared and a decision is made in one flowchart block several instructions will be required to perform those functions. One method of comparing the real data with the ideal data is to subtract one from the other. Since subtraction affects the status flags the branch instructions could then choose the proper correction routine. If subtraction is used, however, the original data will be lost as the difference replaces it in the accumulator. The data could be and perhaps is duplicated in memory allowing it to be reloaded into the accumulator for use in the correction routine. Several instructions can be saved if the compare instruction is used. Described as A − M, the CMP subtracts the contents of a memory location from an accumulator, affecting the flags, but does not store the difference in the accumulator. The difference is forgotten, the original data remains in the accumulator and a decision can be made about the appropriate correction routine.

Making that decision requires more than one instruction since a branch instruction that has three alternatives is not available. The CMP will affect the negative flag allowing a BMI instruction to be used for one routine. A BGT can follow to point to the second correction routine. The BPL cannot be used since it considers zero to be positive. Any data that gets past both the BGT and BMI can be assumed equal to the ideal data. This scheme is flowcharted in Fig. 8-8.

The program constantly monitors the process; when it finishes one correction routine it restarts, looking at the condi-

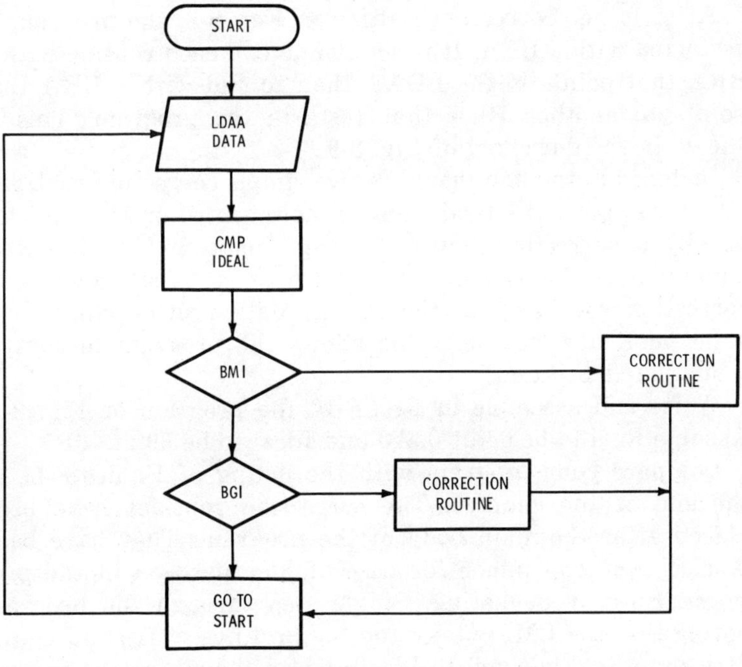

Fig. 8-8. The compare and decide routine.

tion of the process and making needed corrections. A program that operates on data as it is available from a process is called real time processing.

The Branch Always instruction can be used to restart the program. The BRA does not examine or depend on any conditions; the branch is always taken. In this program, the branch will be back to the LDAA. Notice that since this branch is backwards in the program the offset will be negative. As any negative number, a negative offset must be in two's complement form.

Before the program is written, the BGT and BMI must be defined in terms of which condition, higher or lower than the ideal, they will catch. The CMP subtracts the ideal from the real data and the flags are set accordingly. If the real is larger than the ideal data, the negative flag will not be set, if the ideal is larger than the real, the negative flag will be set. The BMI then is taken when the real data is too low and the process must be increased. The BPL is taken when the real data is too high and the process must be decreased.

After either correction routine in Fig. 8-8, the program is restarted with a BRA. It is simpler to end each routine with a BRA that points to the LDAA than to end with a BRA that points to another BRA that restarts the program. This is shown in the flowchart of Fig. 8-9.

Included in the flowchart are two simple correction routines. Called ramping, the Real value is incremented or decremented one by a correction routine. Using this technique the Real value will gradually inch up or down to the Ideal value. Both correction routines and the correct data routine store their value in Real's location. This allows the program to control a simulated process.

Write and assemble in Fig. 8-10 the program of Fig. 8-9. Assume Real to be 04 at 00A0 and Ideal to be 09 at 00B0.

Compare your program with the listing of Figure 8-11 at the end of the chapter. The correction routines have been placed after the main body of the program. They have been labeled over and under for ease of identification in the program. Enter your listing. Single step through the program noting that the BMI is taken on the first five passes. After the fifth pass Real is equal to Ideal and on the sixth pass neither the BMI or BGT is taken. Change Real to 0A and single step

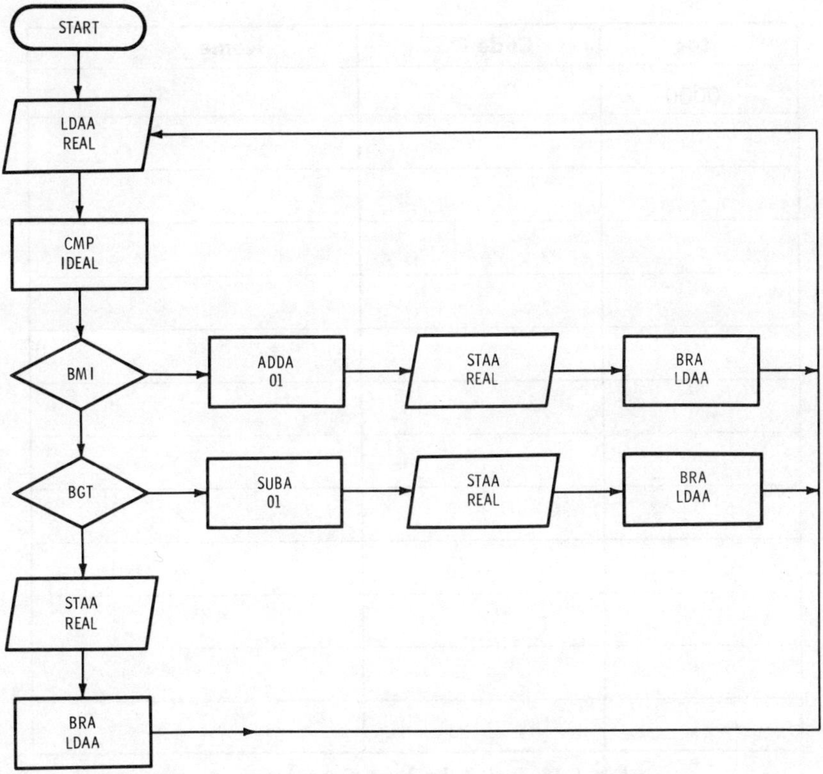

Fig. 8-9. Real time control of a simulated process.

through the program again. When Real is greater than Ideal the BGT is taken until Real equals Ideal. Changing Real simulates changes that naturally occur during the process. Change Real to AE and run the program at the processor's clock speed. Since the program continually examines the process a jump to monitor was not included. The process will continue to be examined until you stop execution and return to the monitor by pressing the reset button. Running at between 0.5 and 2.0 megahertz the processor will correct Real faster than you can press the reset. List the value of Real ______.

In developing the program, each correction routine included an STAA that replaces the original with the corrected Real and a BRA to LDAA, which restarts the program. An alternative solution would omit the STAA and end each correction routine with a BRA to the STAA at 0008, which would replace

Loc	Code	Name
0000		

Fig. 8-10. Write the Real Time program.

Real and restart the program. The alternative would require less program memory since just one STAA serves all options, but it would take longer to execute since an additional BRA is executed getting from a correction routine to the STAA at 0008.

Most programs include one or more branch instructions. Since all branch instructions require the relative addressing mode, a program that would calculate the offsets used would be valuable. The program could simply subtract the PC from the destination. Such a program is flowcharted in Fig. 8-12.

Write and assemble the program in Fig. 8-13. Assume the programmer must load the destination address at 00C0, the PC at 00C1, and can find the offset at 00C2. Compare your program with the listing of Fig. 8-14 at the end of the chapter.

Use the program to verify the offsets used in the Real Time program of Fig. 8-11. Two cautions must be observed when

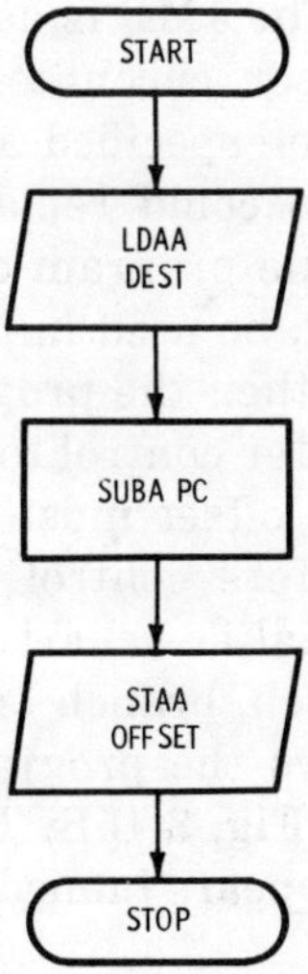

Fig. 8-12. An offset calculation program.

using the offset calculator. If a branch crosses a page in the forward direction, from 00F6 to 010A, the higher address should be entered first since only the low address bytes are used. The maximum allowable forward offset is +127 bytes and the maximum backward offset is −128 bytes. This program is fully relocatable; it can be placed anywhere in memory.

Loc	Code	Name
0000		

Fig. 8-13. Writing the offset program.

It would seem that the use of relative addressing severely limits the processor's ability to transfer control. If a branch of greater than 127 bytes is desired, the branch instruction can be used with the jump instruction and any location in memory is accessible. The JMP instruction causes the contents of the PC to be replaced with the two bytes that immediately follow it. The JMP is not a conditional instruction; every time the processor encounters a JMP, program control is transferred to the specified address and execution continues. Jump instructions could replace the branch always instructions in the real time program of Fig. 8-11. Since the jump must, for the present, be used in the absolute mode, replacing the BRAs would lengthen the program by three bytes.

To transfer control to a destination out of a branch's range, the branch offset must point the processor to a JMP which then transfers control to the desired location. This is shown in the partial flowchart of Fig. 8-15A. Using the opposite condition branch, branch on carry set instead of branch on carry clear, allows the programmer to follow the branch with the JMP as in Fig. 8-15B. This scheme is usually preferable since the JMP appears immediately after the branch in the program listing.

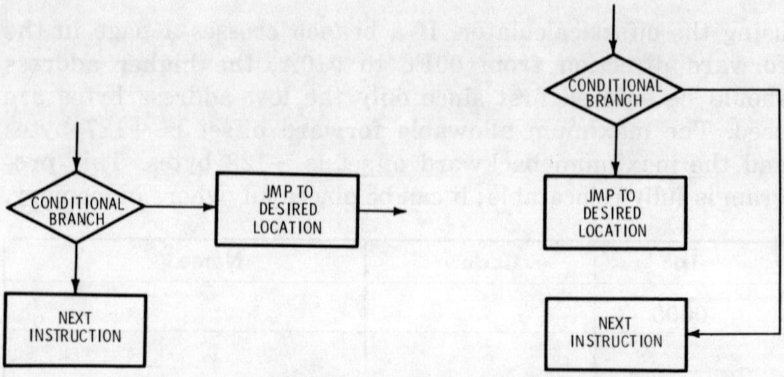

(A) Branch on carry clear. *(B) Branch on carry set.*

Fig. 8-15. Using the JMP with a conditional branch.

The wide variety of conditional branch instructions available to the programmer allows easy testing of any condition. Many of the branch instructions rely on the zero flag. Occupying bit position 2 in the CCR, the zero flag is set when an operation results in 00 and is reset when the result is anything else. As shown on the programmer's card, all of the memory reference instructions affect the Z flag. It makes the greater than, less than, and equal to branches all possible.

An instruction that is useful in checking for a value is the bit test instruction. The BITX performs the logical AND function on an accumulator and a memory location. It affects the flags but, like the CMP, it does not save the result of the AND. Similar to the BITX and the CMP is the test instruction which subtracts 00 from an accumulator, TSTX, or a memory location, TST. Like the BITX and CMP it affects only the flags. These instructions can be used to test for size, sign, or content without destroying the data. They are almost always followed by a branch instruction.

The 6800 provides the programmer with a wide variety of conditional branch instructions that allow the programmer great flexibility in manipulating data. Chapter 9 will discuss another major application of the branch instructions, the loop.

Loc	Code	Name
0000	96 B0	LDAA, direct, B
0002	9B C0	ADDA, direct, C
0004	28 ______	BVC, to STAA
0006	88 80	EORA, immed, 80
0008	97 A0	STAA, direct, A
000A	7E XX XX	JMP, extnd, monitor

Fig. 8-3. The assembled addition program.

Loc	Code	Name
0000	96 B0	LDAA, direct, B
0002	2A 01	BPL, to LDAB
0004	40	NEGA
0005	D6 C0	LDAB, direct, C
0007	2A 01	BPL, to ABA
0009	50	NEGB
000A	1B	ABA
000B	28 02	BVC, to STAA
000D	88 80	EORA, 80
000F	97 A0	STAA, direct, A
0011	7E XX XX	JMP, extnd, monitor

Fig. 8-6. The assembled addition program.

Loc	Code	Name
0000	96 A0	LDAA, direct, Real
0002	91 B0	CMPA, direct, Ideal
0004	2B 06	BMI, under correction
0006	2E 0A	BGT, over correction
0008	97 A0	STAA, direct, Real
000A	20 F4	BRA, LDAA
000C	8B 01	ADDA, immed, 01 under
000E	97 A0	STAA, direct, Real
0010	20 EE	BRA, LDAA
0012	80 01	SUBA, immed, 01 over
0014	97 A0	STAA, direct, Real
0016	20 E8	BRA, LDAA

Fig. 8-11. The assembled Real Time program.

Loc	Code	Name
0000	96 C0	LDAA, direct, Dest
0002	90 C1	SUBA, direct, PC
0004	97 C2	STAA, direct, Offset
0006	7E XX XX	JMP, extnd, monitor

Fig. 8-14. The assembled offset calculator.

CHAPTER 9

Loops

Applications from games to checkbooks and from averaging to bulk mailings involve repetition of a group of functions. The programmable loop, using the flags and branch instructions, can make repetitious jobs short and simple.

Objectives

You will be able to:

1. Write count up and count down loop programs
2. Write multiply and divide programs
3. Use indexed addressing
4. Write a program relocator

Although the 6800 does not have a multiply instruction, it would be unreasonable to assume that multiplication will never be needed. Multiplication is shortcut addition and can be replaced with multiple addition—$4 \times 7 = 7 + 7 + 7 + 7$ or $4 \times 7 = 4 + 4 + 4 + 4 + 4 + 4 + 4$. Generally, $X \times Y$ means Y is added to itself X times or X added to itself Y times. A program that multiplies 7 times 5 is shown in Fig. 9-1.

While this approach will work it is not the most desirable. A unique routine must be written for each pair of numbers that can be multiplied and as the numbers get larger the routines become unbearably long. Imagine the program to multiply 87 by 61! Multiplication by repeated addition is a perfect loop application.

A programmable loop consists of the operations needed for the desired function, a location called a counter, a statement that controls the counter, and a conditional branch statement. Fig. 9-2 shows a loop multiplication program for X × Y.

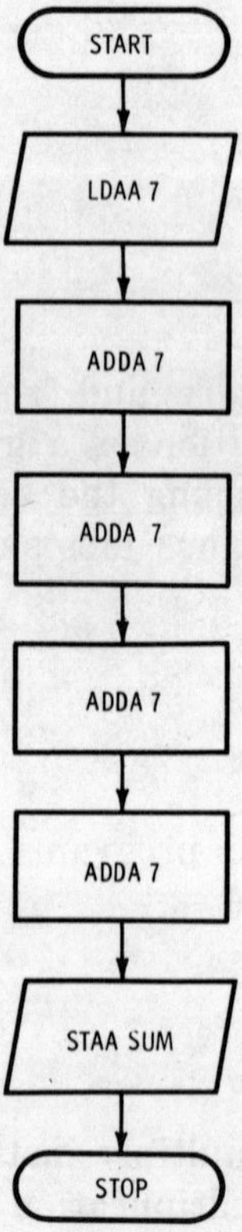

Fig. 9-1. Multiplication by repeated addition flowchart.

In this program the ADDA is the function desired for multiplication. The Y serves as the counter and the DEC controls it. The BNE causes the looping action.

Initially the CLRA replaces the contents of accumulator A with zero. The clear instruction can be used on either accumulator, CLRX, or a memory location, CLR. It performs the function of a LDAX 00 or STAX 00 but requires only one byte of program memory. Accumulator A must be cleared before the ADDA adds X to it.

Each time X is added to the accumulator, the counter, location Y, must be reduced by one. The decrement instruction subtracts one from either accumulator, DECX, or a memory

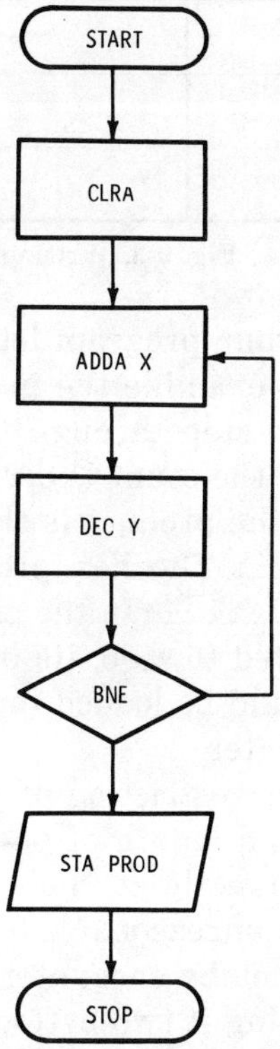

Fig. 9-2. A multiplication-loop program flowchart.

location, DEC. After the counter is reduced, the BNE examines the zero flag to determine whether the process is complete. When X is added Y times, the counter reaches zero and the branch is not taken so the program continues.

Write and assemble in Fig. 9-3 the multiplication program. Assume X to be at location 00A0, Y to be at location 00A1 and the product to be at location 00A2. Compare your program with the listing of Fig. 9-4 at the end of the chapter.

Loc	Code	Name

Fig. 9-3. Writing the multiplication program.

Enter your program letting X = 2 and Y = 3. Run the program and examine the product, 6. Change X to 7 and Y to 4 and single step through the program. Notice that each time 7 is added the count is decremented. After 4 additions the loop ends and the product is stored. Examine and record the product ______. The hex product of 7 × 4 is 1C. Examine and record Y ______. In the process of using Y as a counter it was decremented to zero, its original value lost. To save the value of Y it could be loaded into accumulator B which would serve as the counter.

A major restriction of this program is the limitation of its product to a length of one byte. Two numbers cannot be multiplied correctly if their product is longer than eight bits. Since it is unreasonable to assume that a product greater than 256 will not be encountered the product should be expanded. By assigning it two bytes, a 16-bit product can be handled and two single byte numbers cannot be multiplied to produce a product longer than two bytes. Expansion of the program involves detecting each carry and adding it to the most significant byte of the product. Fig. 9-5 contains a flowchart of extended multiplication.

The BCC detects a carry and adds 1 to the product's most significant byte, stored in ACCB. Write and assemble in Fig. 9-6 the multiplication program.

Compare your program with the listing of Fig. 9-7 at the end of the chapter. Enter your program letting X be 4 at

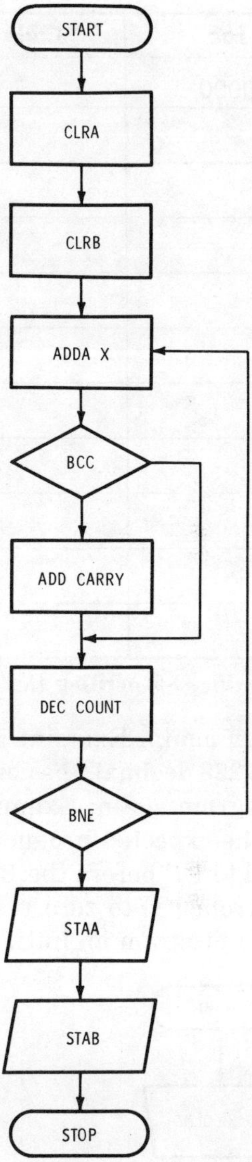

Fig. 9-5. Multiplication with a two-byte product flowchart.

00A0, Y be 3 at 00A1, and the product be at 00A2, LSB, and 00A3, MSB.

Run the program and examine the product. The high byte contains 00, as it should. Change X to 10 and Y to 10 and run the program again. Examine and record the product ______. The product 256 appears as 0100. Change Y to 12 and run the

Loc	Code	Name
0000		

Fig. 9-6. Writing the extended multiplication program.

program again. Examine and record the product ______. Hex 0120 is 288 decimal, the correct product. Change Y to 0 and run the program again. Examine and record the product. ______. Zero, the expected product, is not listed because Y was decremented to FF before the BNE examined it. The count then ran down from FF to zero resulting in the 1000 product. To correct the program an initial zero must be detected.

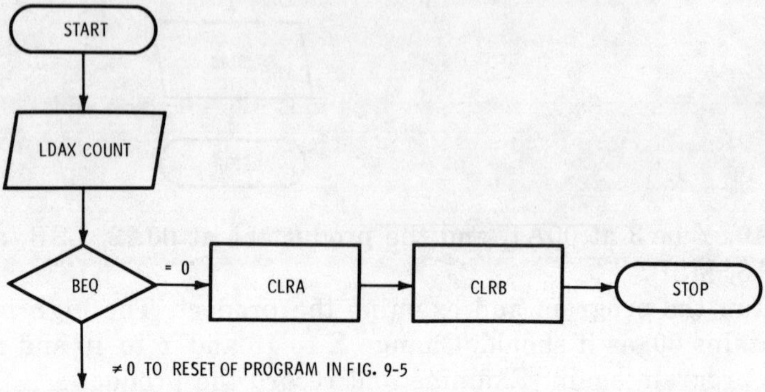

Fig. 9-8. Detecting multiplication by zero flowchart.

Any operation that will affect the zero flag, but not the count, can be used. The initial count could be loaded into either accumulator, affecting the zero flag. A BEQ would follow with the branch going to instructions that would make the product zero and end the program. Zero must be detected before the loop begins, as shown in Fig. 9-8.

Although the multiplication program will work, it may not be efficient in terms of the processor's time. Multiplying a number by zero does not require much time but multiplying by FF runs the program 256 times. A generally more efficient and widely used multiplication scheme is shown in Fig. 9-9.

```
     47
  × 100
  -----
      0
     0    shifted left one place
   47     multiplied and shifted left one place
  -----
   4700   product is sum of multiplications
```

Fig. 9-9. Multiplying 100 by 47.

Based on Booth's algorithm, multiplication is performed in the same way you would multiply 47 and 100. In multiplying 47 and 100 a zero is recorded since 100's least significant digit is zero. A second zero is recorded below and one place left of the first zero since 100's next most significant digit is zero. Below and one digit left of the second zero 47 is recorded, the result of multiplying one and 47. Finally all three numbers, two zeros and the shifted 47 are added to obtain the product, 4700.

By using this same technique two binary numbers can be multiplied. Fig. 9-10 shows the multiplication of binary 101 and 10. The process begins with the multiplication of 101 by 0 with a result of zero. 101 is then multiplied by 1 and the

```
   101    multiplicand
  × 10    multiplier
  ----
     0    zero is result of multiplication by zero
  101     multiplied and shifted
  ----
  1010    product is sum of multiplications
```

Fig. 9-10. Binary multiplication.

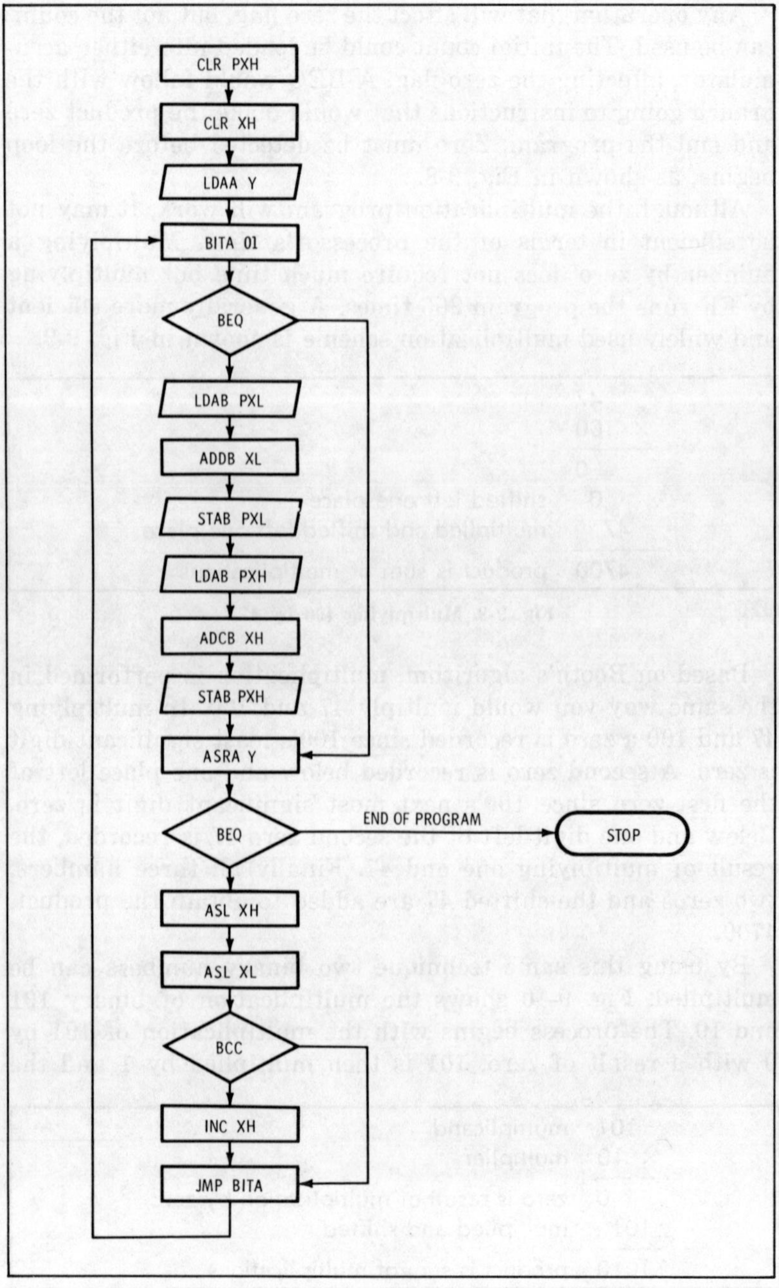

Fig. 9-11. Implementing fast multiplication flowchart.

result, 101, is recorded one bit position left. The product is the sum of the multiplications. Generally, multiplication by zero always results in zero and multiplication by one results in the original number.

Implementing this algorithm is not difficult. Each bit of the multiplier must be examined in turn. If it is one, the multiplicand is added to the product; if it is zero, a zero is added. In either case, the multiplicand is shifted left and the multiplier shifted right. After the last bit has been examined the multiplication is completed. One way of performing this add and shift technique is shown in Fig. 9-11.

Accumulator A is loaded with the multiplier and the least significant bit is added with 01 to determine if it is 1 or 0. If

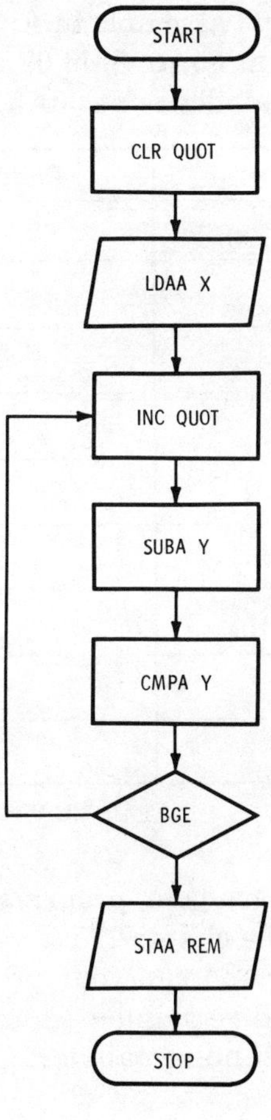

Fig. 9-12. Simple division flowchart.

it is 1, the multiplicand X is added to the product; if it is zero, nothing is added to the product. The multiplier is shifted right and the BEQ checks for the end of the process by examining the zero flag. If it is set, the multiplier is zero indicating the end of the multiplication. If it is not set, both bytes of the multiplicand, X, are shifted left and the next bit of the multiplier is tested as the loop starts again. This is not the only possible nor the most efficient coding of multiplication using Booth's algorithm.

Division can be done in the same manner as multiplication using repeated subtraction instead of addition. A program that divides X by Y is shown in Fig. 9-12.

The program simply subtracts Y from X repeatedly incrementing the quotient. The remainder is saved and stored. Write and assemble in Fig. 9-13 the division program. Assume X is 10 at 00A0, Y is 02 at 00A1, the quotient is at 00A2 and the remainder is at 00A3.

Loc	Code	Name
0000		

Fig. 9-13. Writing the division program.

Compare your program with the listing of Fig. 9-14 at the end of the chapter.

Enter and run your program. Examine and record the quotient and remainder ______. The quotient of 16 divided by 2 is 8 with no remainder. Change Y to 4 and run the program again. Examine and record the quotient and remainder ______. The proper quotient is 4. Change Y to 5 and run the program again. Examine and record the quotient and the remainder ______. Sixteen divided by five is, of course, three with a remainder of one. Division can be performed with Booth's algorithm using the same shift and add technique.

Many loop applications involve batch processing, performing the same operations on data in many memory locations. These applications range from payroll generators to search routines to checkbook balancers. Most useful in these applications is indexed addressing.

Like other modes, indexed addressing specifies the location of data to be used by an operation. Notice on the programmer's card that most memory and accumulator operations can use the indexed mode. Indexed addressing depends on a 16-bit user controlled register located on the 6800 chip called the index register. The data address is specified as a combination of the contents of the index register and an offset that follows the instruction.

The index register is somewhat like an accumulator; its contents can be loaded from or stored in memory, incremented or decremented, or compared with the contents of a memory location. Since it is a two byte, 16-bit register, the index register must be loaded from or stored in two memory locations.

The contents of the address that follows an LDX is loaded into the high byte of the index register. The low byte of the index register is loaded with the contents of the memory byte that follows the one listed after the LDX. If an LDX direct is followed with A0 the contents of A0 are loaded into the register's high byte and the contents of A1 are loaded into the register's low byte. If an STX direct is followed by A0 the high byte of the register is stored at A0 and the low byte of the register is stored at A1. An INX or DEX adds 01 to or subtracts 01 from the contents of the register.

The index register can be used effectively by loading it with the beginning address of a table, a group of related bytes to be used in an operation. The offset can then be used to point to each entry in the table, being incremented after the operation is performed on the current entry. Suppose a group of numbers, perhaps measurements, is acquired by the processor and the average is desired. The average is calculated by adding the numbers and then dividing the sum by the size of the group. The average of 4, 7, 3, 5, 5, and 6 is their sum, 30, divided by the group size, 6. Their average is 5. A program to calculate the average of a group of numbers is flowcharted in Fig. 9-15.

Use of indexed addressing here has several advantages. Each number is added in turn to the sum by means of the

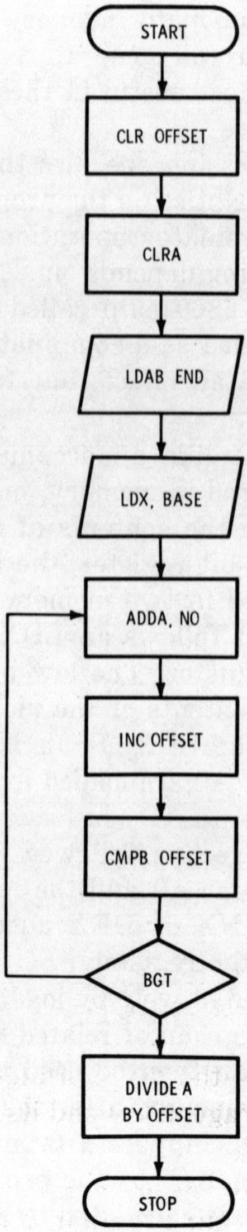

Fig. 9-15. An averaging program flowchart.

offset. The offset can also be compared with the number of table entries which is loaded into accumulator B to indicate the end of the table. The offset is also the number by which the sum is divided. Write and assemble in Fig. 9-16 the averaging program. Assume that the table has eight consecutive entries, beginning at base 0090. Let the table contain the numbers 4, 3, 6, 9, A, 3, 5, and 8. Use the division algorithm developed in Fig. 9-13. Store the average at A2 and its remainder at A3.

Loc	Code	Name
0000		

Fig. 9-16. Writing the average program.

Compare your program with the listing of Fig. 9-17 at the end of the chapter. Enter and run your program. Examine and record the average ______. Since the calculated average is 6 the remainder is zero.

If the number of entries in the table is not known, or variable, the program can be altered to detect the end of the table. A special character recognized by the program serves to mark the end of the table and is placed after the last number in it. This character cannot appear as a regular entry in the table since it would prematurely end the summing process. It must, then, be disallowed either naturally or by the programmer. The end character is loaded into accumulator B and the CMPB is used in the indexed mode, checking each number in the table. The proper branch statement is the BNE. Make the changes necessary to designate FF as the end of the table character and add it to the listing. Run the program again and examine the average. It should be unchanged.

If a program should involve building a table in memory, a block of locations might need to be cleared. Again, use of the indexed addressing mode can be advantageous. A program that will clear a desired number of locations is flowcharted in Fig. 9-18.

The brevity and speed of this program is a result of using the CLR instruction in the indexed mode. The desired number

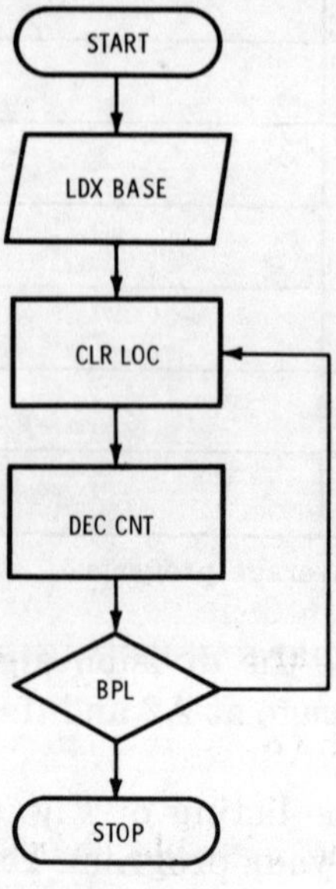

Fig. 9-18. A memory clear program flowchart.

of cleared locations is used as the index offset and also serves as the loop counter. Notice that a count down loop is used. The program clears the highest location first, the offset is decremented and the next lower location is cleared. When the offset is zero the branch is not taken and the program ends. Write and assemble in Fig. 9-19 the memory clear program.

Loc	Code	Name

Fig. 9-19. Writing the memory clear program.

Assume a block of 1A locations beginning at 0040 will be cleared. Compare your program with the listing of Fig. 9-20 at the end of the chapter. Enter and run your program. Examine locations 0040 through 005A, they should all be cleared.

A program may need to search through a table looking for a desired value. The index register allows the search program of Fig. 9-21 to be relatively simple.

This program does not make use of indexed addressing as before. Although the CMPA Loc operation is in the indexed mode the offset is always zero. Instead of incrementing the offset, the index register itself is incremented so it always contains the address of the byte just examined. If the desired value is found, its location can be identified easily by storing the index register in FND. The program examines the entire table listing all of the locations that contain the desired value. It also examines a table of undetermined length, stopping when it encounters an end of the table character. Write and assemble in Fig. 9-22 the search program.

Assume that FND begins at 00A0, the table's base address is at 00B0 and 00B1, the desired value is at 00B2, and the end character is at 00B3. Let the end of table character be FF.

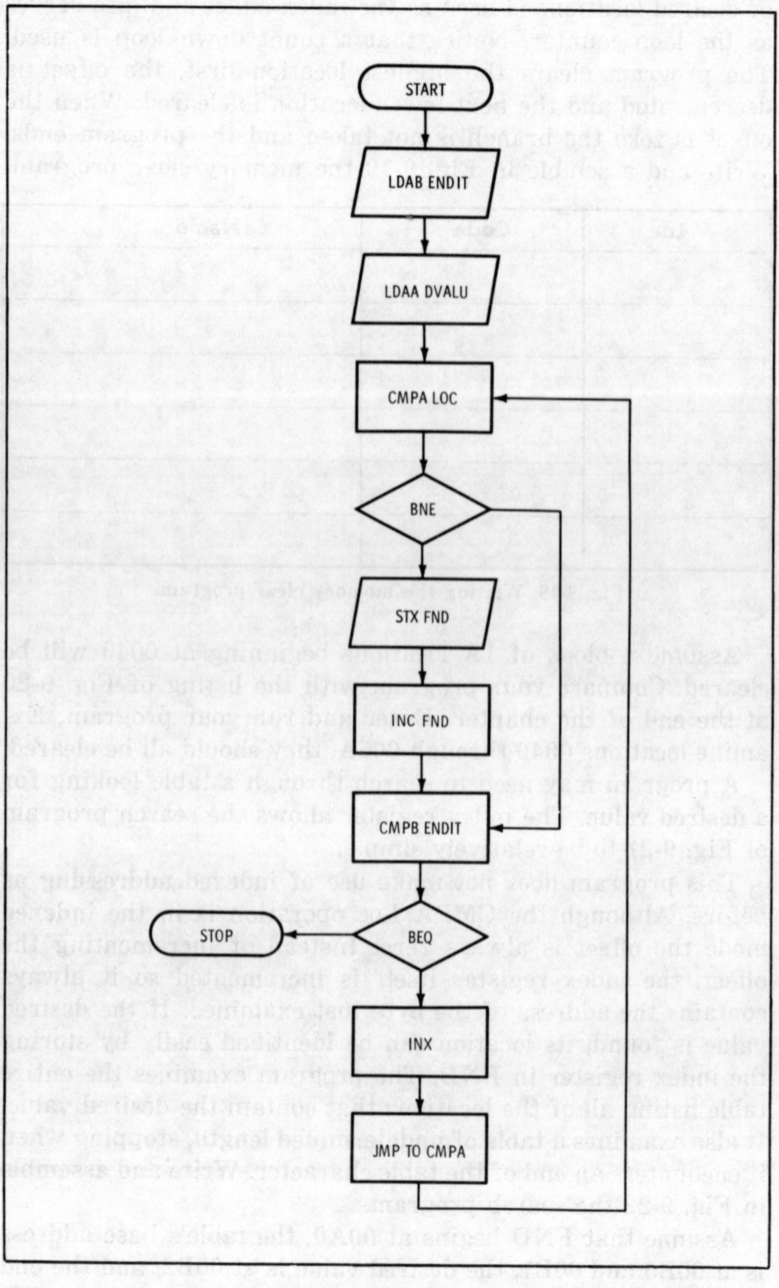

Fig. 9-21. A search program flowchart.

Compare your program with the listing of Fig. 9-23 at the end of the chapter. Enter your program and let it search for 7C starting at location 0000 and ending at 0020. You must enter the end of table character at 0021.

Loc	Code	Name
0000		

Fig. 9-22. Writing the search program.

The program should find a 7C at 000C and at 000F. Change the desired value to 00, reset the FND location and run the program again. All five 00's should be listed. A search program of this type can be used to find both alphanumeric and numeric data. It can be used to produce all the males, females, rich, poor, delinquent customers, residents of New York, or any other identifiable group from a list. It can serve as the basis of a mailing list, billing, or sorting programs. In such applications the program would print the bill, address label, or name

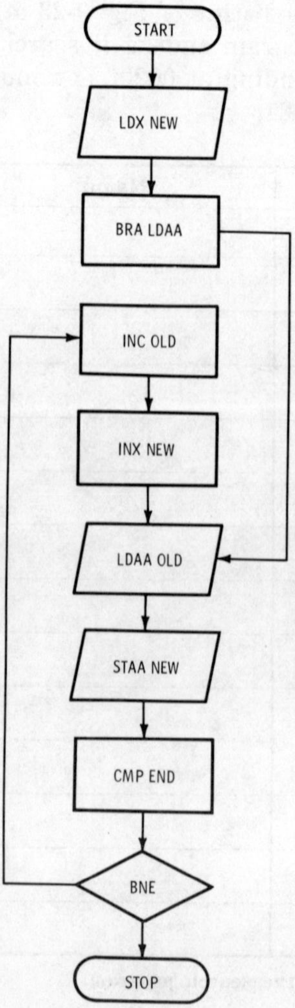

Fig. 9-24. A program relocator flowchart.

on a list instead of just listing the memory address of the desired data.

All of the programs developed have been on the low end of page zero. It might be desirable to keep some programs in the processor for instant use, perhaps a favorite game or the off-set calculator. If programs are developed at the low end of page zero the favorites must be moved to higher locations. The program in Fig. 9-24, called a program relocator, makes use of indexed addressing to move a block of memory to new locations.

The program is quite simple. A memory byte is loaded into the accumulator from an old location and stored in a new location indicated by the index register. Data bytes are moved until the end character, FF, is encountered. Write and assemble in Fig. 9-25 the relocator.

By using the LDAA in the absolute mode and incrementing the index register, data can be moved from or to any addressable locations. Compare your program with the listing of Fig. 9-26 at the end of the chapter.

Loc	Code	Name

Fig. 9-25. Writing the relocator program.

Enter and run your program having it move itself to an area whose base location is 00D0. Examine the bytes following 00D0 to confirm a successful move. Using the new listing at 00D0 move the original listing to an area whose base location is 0030. Examine the bytes following 0030 to confirm the move. The move was undoubtedly unsuccessful and the listing at 00D0 may even be changed. The relocator program itself is not fully relocatable.

A fully relocatable program can be moved to a new area in memory and run successfully without modifications. The modifications needed in a program not fully relocatable are usually address changes that reflect the move. Generally any instruction in the direct, extended, or indexed mode that uses data within the program, as do the INC at 0005 and the CMPA at 000E, must have its address byte modified. Instructions using the relative mode need not be modified since the offset is relative. Change 0006 to DB and 000F to E5 and attempt to move the original list to 0030. Examine the bytes following 0030 to confirm a successful move.

One very important loop application has yet to be covered. The timing loop builds on the basic loop structures just discussed.

Loc	Code	Name
0000	4F	CLRA
0001	9B A0	ADDA, direct X
0003	7A 00 A1	DEC, extnd, Y
0006	26 F9	BNE, to ADDA
0008	97 A2	STAA, direct, Product
000A	7E XX XX	JMP, extnd, to monitor

Fig. 9-4. The assembled multiplication program.

Loc	Code	Name
0000	4F	CLRA
0001	5F	CLRB
0002	9B A0	ADDA, X
0004	24 02	BCC, to DEL
0006	CB 01	ADDB, 01
0008	7A 00 A1	DEC, Y
000B	26 F5	BNE, to ADDA
000D	97 A2	STAA, low byte product
000F	D7 A3	STAB, high byte product
0011	7E XX XX	JMP, to monitor

Fig. 9-7. The assembled extended multiplication program.

Loc	Code	Name
0000	7F 00 A2	CLR, extnd, Quot
0003	96 A0	LDAA, direct, X
0005	7C 00 A2	INC, extnd, Quot
0008	90 A1	SUBA, direct, Y
000A	91 A1	CMPA, direct, Y
000C	2C F7	BGE, to INC
000E	97 A3	STAA, direct, REM
0010	7E XX XX	JMP, extnd, to monitor

Fig. 9-14. The assembled division program.

Loc	Code	Name
0000	7F 00 09	CLR, extnd, offset
0003	4F	CLRA
0004	C6 08	LDAB, immed, End No
0006	DE 9A	LDX, direct, Base
0008	AB 00	ADDA, index, No
000A	7C 00 09	Inc, extnd, offset
000D	D1 09	CMPB, direct, offset
000F	2E F7	BGT, to ADDA
0011	7F 00 A2	CLR, extnd, Aver
0014	7C 00 A2	INC, extnd, Aver
0017	90 09	SUBA, direct, offset
0019	91 09	CMPA, direct, offset
001B	2C F7	BGE, to INC
001D	97 A3	STAA, direct, REM
001F	7E XX XX	JMP, extnd, to monitor

Fig. 9-17. The assembled average program.

Loc	Code	Name
0000	CE 00 40	LDX, immed, Base
0003	6F 1A	CLR, index, Loc
0005	7A 00 04	DEC, extnd, offset
0008	2A F9	BRL, to CLR
000A	7E XX XX	JMP, extnd, to monitor

Fig. 9-20. The assembled memory clear program.

Loc	Code	Name
0000	D6 B3	LDAB, direct, Endit
0002	DE B0	LDX, direct, BASE
0004	96 B2	LDAA, direct, DVAL
0006	A1 00	CMPA, index, 00
0008	26 08	BNE, to CPX
000A	DF A0	STX, direct, FND
000C	7C 00 0B	INC, extnd, LOFND
000F	7C 00 0B	INC, extnd, LOFND
0012	E1 00	CMPB, index, ENDIT
0014	27 04	BEQ, to STOP
0016	08	INX
0017	7E 00 06	JMP, extnd, to CMPA
001A	7E XX XX	JMP, extnd, to monitor STOP

Fig. 9-23. The assembled search program.

Loc	Code	Name
0000	CE ___ ___	LDX, immed, NEW BASE
0003	20 04	BRA, to LDAA
0005	7C 00 0B	INC, extnd, OLD BASE
0008	08	INX, NEW
0009	B6 ___ ___	LDAA, extnd, old
000A	A7 00	STAA, index, new
000E	91 15	CMPA, direct, END
0010	26 F3	BNE, to INC
0012	7E XX XX	JMP, extnd, to monitor
0015	FF	

Fig. 9-26. The assembled relocator program.

CHAPTER 10

Timing Loops

Although the 6800 is relatively slow in the computer world it is unbelievably fast in the human world. Addition in two millionths of a second is not a commonplace human activity! When a processor deals with a human it must allow some time for human reaction and response. Many applications require that it serve as a timer to control a process. The loop is a good way for a processor to waste time. Timing loops will be found in everything from teleprinter circuits to microwave ovens, and from video games to traffic lights.

Objectives

You will be able to:

1. Write a simple timing loop
2. Perform timing loop calculations
3. Write a programmable timer

A simple loop is shown in Fig. 10-1. After the contents of location CNT are loaded into accumulator A it is decremented to zero and the program ends. The program does nothing except take some time.

The amount of time used by the loop can be easily determined. All instructions in the 6800 set require a certain number of machine cycles. A machine cycle is a basic operating routine the processor uses to execute any instruction. The length, in time, of a machine cycle is dependent on the clock frequency or speed. The clock of a processor is a square wave generator that feeds it two out-of-phase signals called clock pulses. A clock generator may be as simple as a dual astable multivibrator IC, the 74123, or it can be a crystal controlled clock module such as the 6871 which is a member of the 6800 family. The 6802 processor has the clock circuitry built on the MPU and only a resistor and capacitor are required externally.

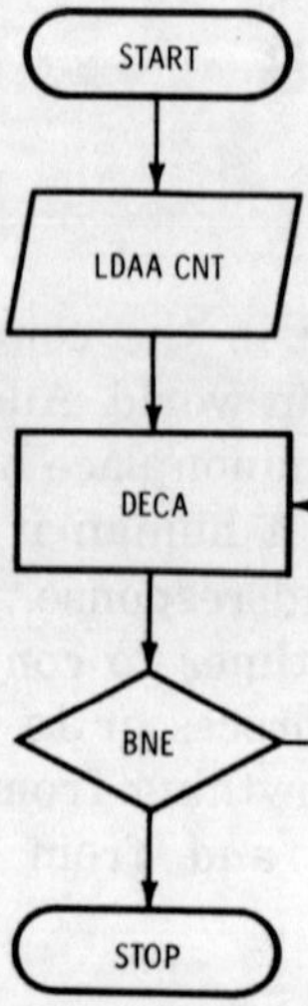

Fig. 10-1. A simple loop flowchart.

The control unit uses the constant clock signals as a base from which it can synchronize all of the actions of the processor. If the clock signals are removed, the processor cannot function. The 6800 can accept clock signals from around 500 kHz to 1 MHz. A higher clock speed allows the processor to act faster. The clock frequency is inversely related to the length of a machine cycle, cy = 1/F. If a clock of a processor is running at 1 MHz, its cycle is 1 μs long. (M is 10^6 or 1,000,000, μ is 10^{-6} or 1/1,000,000). If a clock of a processor is running at 500 kHz, its cycle is 2 μs. Information about the speed at which your processor runs is included in the system description. In the examples that follow a 1-MHz clock speed is assumed.

The center column of the programmer's card, marked ~, lists the number of clock cycles each instruction requires. An LDAX requires 4 cycles in the extended mode and 3 cycles in the direct mode. Notice that generally instructions used in the inherent and immediate modes require the fewest cycles and instructions used in the extended mode and the indexed mode require the most.

A simple addition program is shown in Fig. 10-2 and is assembled in Fig. 10-3.

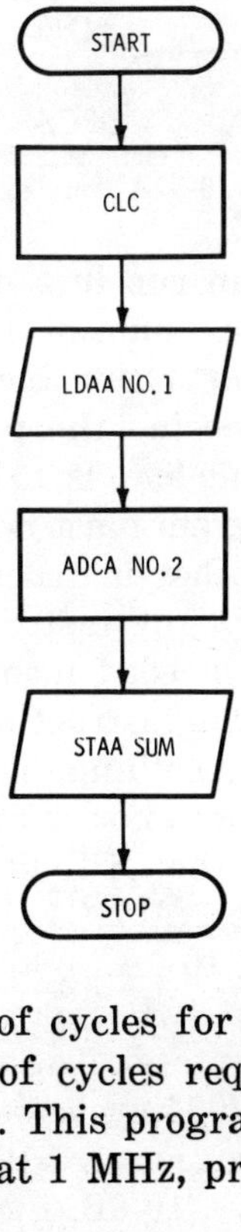

Fig. 10-2. A simple addition flowchart.

A column that lists the number of cycles for each instruction has been added. The number of cycles required by this program is the sum of that column. This program runs in 16 cycles. If the processor is running at 1 MHz, program execution takes 16 μs.

Loop calculations must account for the repetitive action. The program of Fig. 10-1 is assembled in Fig. 10-4.

The number of cycles required by this program is not simply the sum of the cycles of the individual instructions because the BNE and the DECA are repeated. It is obvious that the

LDAA and the JMP will be executed only once during the program so they can be listed. The total is equal to 3 plus loop plus 3. Each pass through the loop the BNE and the DECA are each executed once so they can be listed. Total = 3 + (2 + 4) + 3. The number of times they are performed in the program depends on the number at CNT. If CNT is 10 the expression would become 3 + 10 (2 + 4) + 3 = total. If CNT is 96 the expression would become 3 + 96 (2 + 4) + 3 = total. Generally, the number of cycles required by the program is shown in Fig. 10-5.

3	+	CNT(2	+	4)	+	3	=	Total
LDAA		DECA		BNE		JMP		

Fig. 10-5. A time expression for the loop program.

The loop can run in a minimum of 12 cycles when CNT is 1 and in a maximum of 1542 cycles when CNT is 00 or 256. It can also run in any increment of 6 cycles between the extremes by choosing the proper CNT. The largest time delay afforded by this loop is 1542 μs, or 1.542 thousandths of a second. The program must be altered if a longer delay is desired.

Adding another instruction to the loop would increase the delay possible. Any instruction can be used providing it does not change a needed memory location. It should only waste time. The 6800 instruction set includes an instruction that does just that, nothing. The instruction is called the NOP, no operation, it does not change or alter any memory location or affect any of the CCR flags. Notice that the NOP uses two machine cycles. A NOP has been added to the loop that is shown in Fig. 10-6A.

Adding the NOP makes the timing expression 3 + CNT (2 + 2 + 4) + 3 = total. The maximum delay is now 3 + 256 (2 + 2 + 4) + 3 = 2054 cycles = 2054 μs. The addition of one NOP increased execution by 512 cycles! Including two NOPs in the loop, as in Fig. 10-6B, increases it another 512 cycles to 3 + CNT (2 + 2 + 2 + 4) + 3 = 2566 μs.

Although NOPs are valuable additions to time delay programs there is a practical limit to the number that can be added to a loop. A one-second delay would require a loop containing 3900 NOPs!

A longer delay can be obtained if the CNT is loaded into the index register since it is 16 bits wide. A delay loop that uses the index register is shown in Fig. 10-7.

The expression for this loop is $4 + CNT(4 + 4) + 3$. A maximum delay of $3 + 65536(4 + 4) + 3 = 524294$ μs, half a second, is possible when CNT is 00065536. Adding one NOP increases it by 131072 cycles to $3 + 65536(2 + 4 + 4) + 3 =$

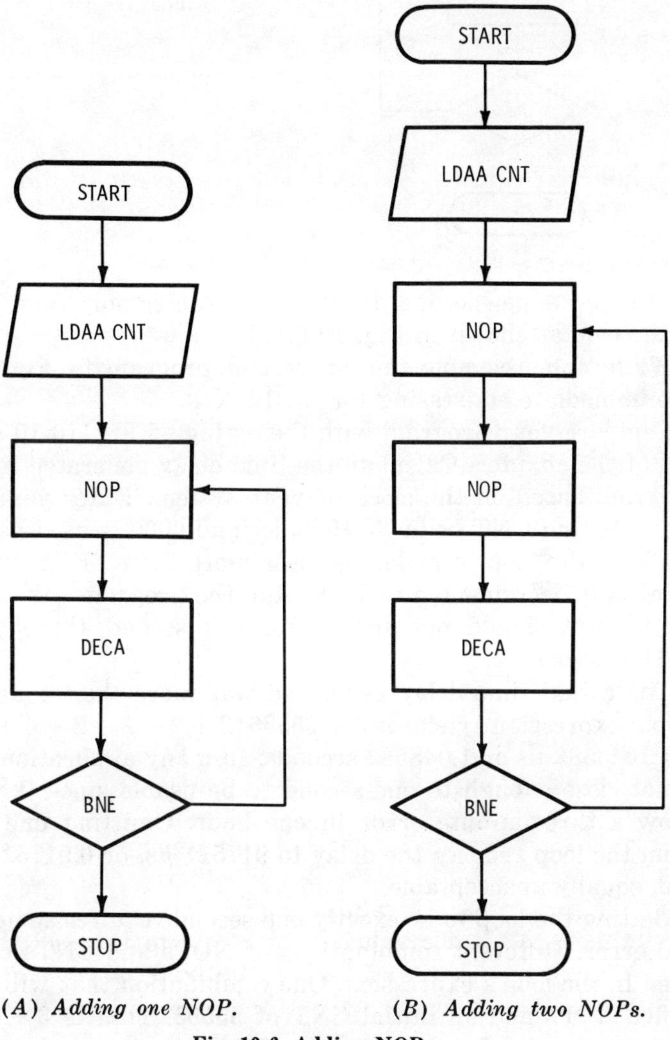

(*A*) *Adding one NOP.* (*B*) *Adding two NOPs.*

Fig. 10-6. Adding NOPs.

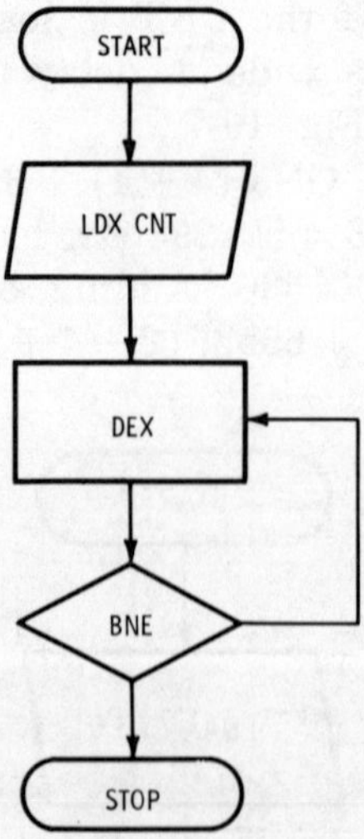

Fig. 10-7. A delay loop in the index register.

655366 μs. A one-second delay would require only four NOPs in the loop as shown in Fig. 10-8.

Write and assemble the one-second program in Fig. 10-9. Use immediate addressing for the LDX.

Compare your program with the listing of Fig. 10-10 at the end of the chapter. Calculate the time delay generated by this program based on the clock of your system. Enter your program, letting CNT be 0000. Hexadecimal 0000 is used because it allows the loop to make one pass more than FFFF since it is initially decremented to FFF. Run the program—the monitor prompt should not appear for one second (based on a 1-MHz clock).

The actual time delay generated was more than 1 μs. The loops expression yields: $3 + 65536(2 + 2 + 2 + 2 + 4 + 4) + 3 = 1048582$ μs or 1.048582 seconds. In many applications this is not close enough to one second to be usable since it would allow a three-minute error in one hour. Omitting one NOP from the loop reduces the delay to 917511 μs, or 0.917511 second, equally unacceptable.

Getting the loop to be exactly one second requires some trial and error. Different combinations of NOPs and CNTs can be tried in the loop's expression. One combination that will work is five NOPs and an initial CNT of 55555. That is $3 + 55555 (2 + 2 + 2 + 2 + 2 + 4 + 4) + 3 = 999996$ μs, just 4 μs less

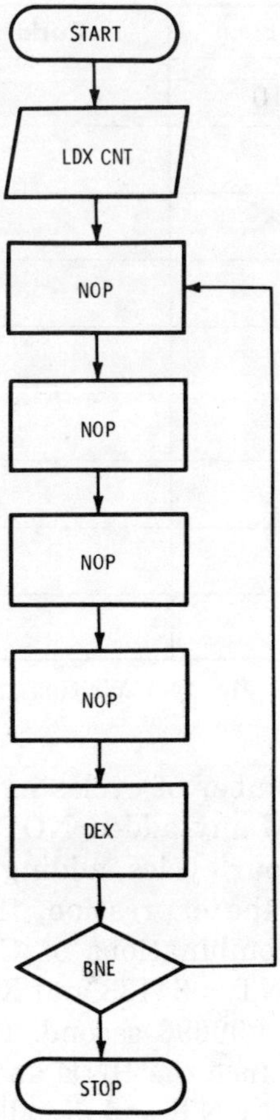

Fig. 10-8. A one-second loop.

than exactly one second. Two NOPs after the loop, just before the JMP, will make the loop exactly one second. Other combinations of NOPs and CNTs may produce a one-second loop.

If your processor does not run at 1 MHz, loop calculations are still simple. The time required for one machine cycle, 1/(clock speed), is multiplied by the total obtained from the loop expression. If the clock speed is 614.6 kHz the time required for one cycle is 1.6271 μs, 1/(614600). The program of Fig. 10-10 then yields a delay of 1048582 cycles $\times$ 1.6271 μs = 1.7061 seconds. Calculation of a one-second delay involves finding the number of NOPs needed in the expression as in Fig. 10-11.

Loc	Code	Name
0010		

Fig. 10-9. Writing the one-second delay program.

The number of cycles in the loop is X, including the DECA, BNE, and any added NOPs. Since the DECA and BNE both require four cycles, adding one NOP makes X = 10. If X = 10 then, by the expression, the delay is 1.06666 seconds. When various combinations of CNT and X are tried the combination of CNT = 34133 and X = 18 gives a delay of 614400 cycles which is .999690 second. If X = 18, five NOPs are needed in the loop since the BNE and DECA use eight. The loop would, using this CNT and X, allow a .01-second error per hour or a one-minute error per 250 days. Other combinations may allow a closer loop.

$$\text{Total} = 3 + 65536(X) + 3$$

$$\frac{1000000\mu s}{1.6271} = 3 + 65536(X) + 3$$

$$614590 = 3 + 65536X + 3$$

$$614584 = 65536(X)$$

$$\frac{614584}{65536} = X$$

$$9.3778 \text{ cycles} = X$$

Fig. 10-11. Calculating a one-second delay.

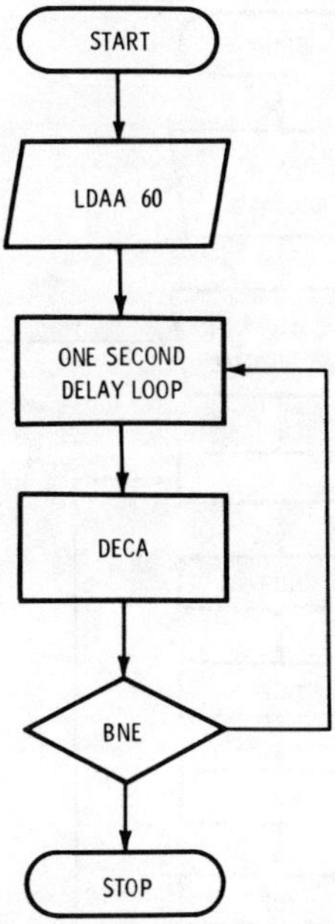

Fig. 10-12. A one-minute delay flowchart.

Using the one-second loop of Fig. 10-10 as a base, a one-minute program can be developed. To extend the delay another loop must be added as shown in Fig. 10-12.

This program has a loop within a loop, called nested loops. Sixty, the number of seconds in a minute, is loaded into ACCA. The one-second loop of Fig. 10-10 is executed and ACCA is decremented to 59. The branch is taken and the one-second loop runs again. A one-second delay occurs each pass through the ACCA loop delay which runs 60 times providing a one-minute delay. The expanded flowchart is shown in Fig. 10-13.

Write and assemble in Fig. 10-14 the one-minute program. Sixty in the ACCA loop and 55555 in the one-second loop must be converted to hex for the program.

Compare your listing with Fig. 10-15 at the end of the chapter. Enter and run your program. The prompt should not be seen until one minute after execution begins.

The one-minute delay can be expanded to a 0–256 minute programmable delay if another loop is added as in Fig. 10-16.

Accumulator B is loaded with the desired delay in minutes. The one-minute loop is executed and ACCB is decremented.

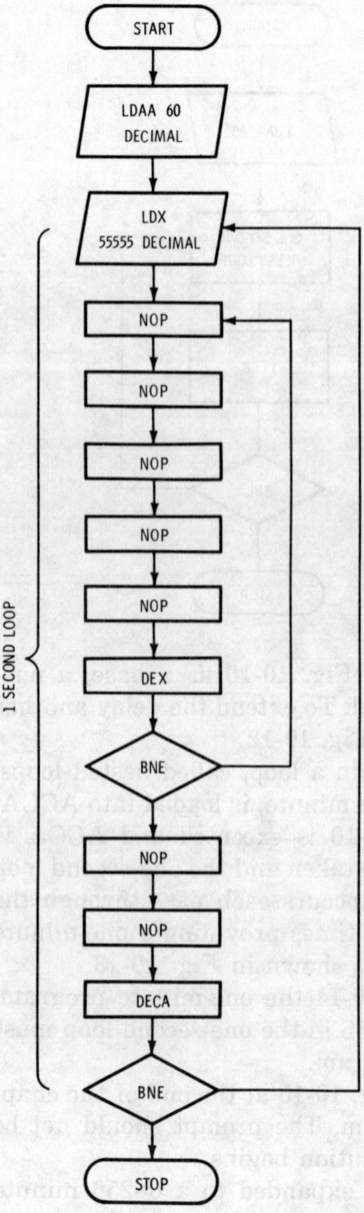

Fig. 10-13. A one-minute delay expanded flowchart.

Loc	Code	Name
000E		

Fig. 10-14. Writing the one-minute loop program.

The branch is taken and the one-minute loop runs again. A one-minute delay is obtained with each pass through the ACCB loop. The expanded flowchart is shown in Fig. 10-17.

Write and assemble in Fig. 10-18 the programmable timer of Fig. 10-17. Notice that only the ACCB loop has not been written before.

Compare your program with the listing of Fig. 10-19 at the end of the chapter. Enter and run the timer, setting the timer for two minutes. The prompt should appear two minutes after execution has begun. Change the number minutes at 000D to 0A and run the program again. The prompt should be seen 10 minutes after execution begins.

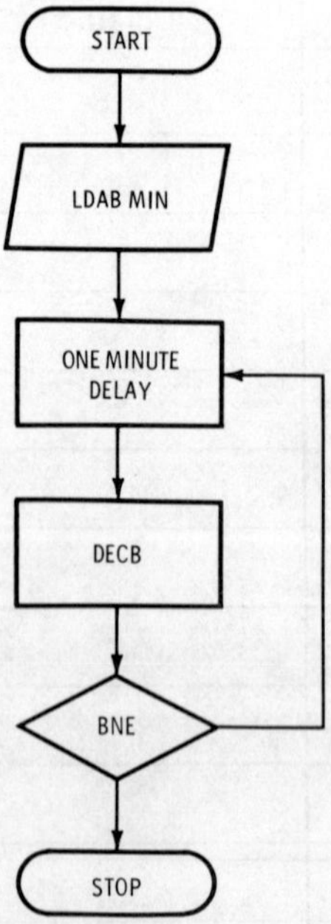

Fig. 10-16. A programmable timer flowchart.

Careful examination of the flowchart of Fig. 10-17 reveals time errors introduced by the addition of the ACCA and the ACCB loops. As each passes through the ACCA six microseconds are added to the total time by the execution of the DECA and BNE. Thirty-six microseconds are added each minute. Another six microseconds are added each minute by the DECB and BNE of the outer loop. A total of 42 microseconds are added each minute, 0.00252 second each hour. If greater accuracy is required the CNT-NOP combination may be adjusted.

Occasionally a programmer must look at a timer loop program and determine the total delay or alter the delay provided. Examine the timer program of Fig. 10-19. Before the delay allowed can be calculated each loop must be identified. Sketch on Fig. 10-19 a line linking the branch of each loop to its destination. The delay provided by each loop must be calculated with an expression. Starting with the innermost loop and expanding in turn to each outer loop write an expression for the program ____

____.
Compare your expression with that of Fig. 10-20. Any delay

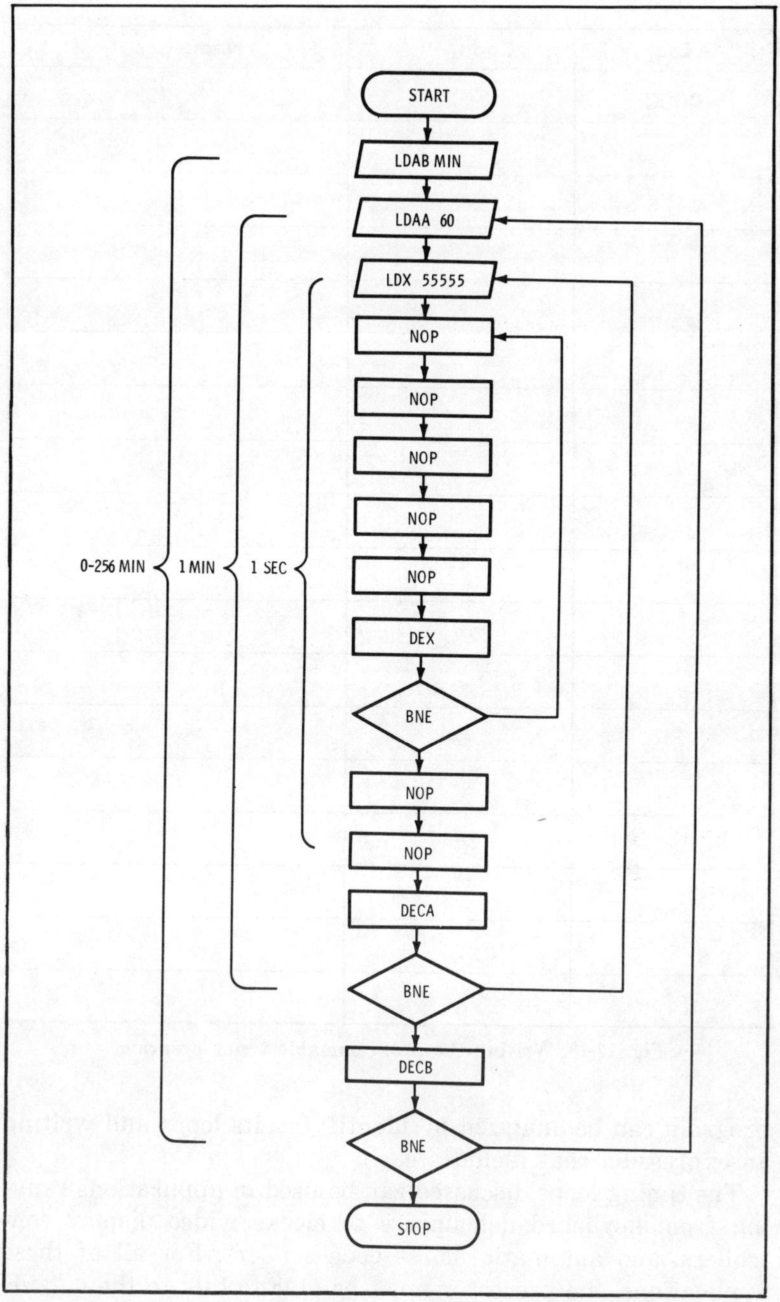

Fig. 10-17. A programmable timer expanded flowchart.

Loc	Code	Name
000C		

Fig. 10-18. Writing the programmable timer program.

program can be analyzed by identifying its loops and writing an expression that includes each.

The timing loops discussed can be used in applications ranging from keyboard debouncers to clocks, video display controllers, and automatic morse code senders. For all of these applications, the processor must be able to talk to the outside world.

```
Time = 2 + 02{2 + 3C[3 + 55555
       LDAB   LDAA      LDX

                  (2 + 2 + 2 + 2 + 2 + 4 + 4)
                        NOP's       DEX   BNE

                     +  2  +   2  +   2  +  4] +  2  +  4}
                       NOP   NOP   DECA   BNE  DECB   BNE
```

Fig. 10-20. Calculated expression of the programmable timer in Fig. 10-19.

Loc	Code	Name	Cyl
0000	0C	CLC	2
0001	96 A0	LDAA, direct, No 1	3
0003	89 FF	ADCA, immed, No 2	2
0005	A7 0C	STAA, index, Sum	6
0007	7E XX XX	JMP, extnd, to monitor	3

Fig. 10-3. The assembled addition program.

Loc	Code	Name	Cyl
0000	96 A0	LDAA, direct, CNT	3
0002	4A	DECA	2
0003	26 FD	BNE, to DECA	4
0005	7E XX XX	JMP, extnd, to monitor	3

Fig. 10-4. The assembled loop program.

Loc	Code	Name
0010	CE 00 00	LDX, immed
0013	01	NOP
0014	01	NOP
0015	01	NOP
0016	01	NOP
0017	09	DEX
0018	26 F9	BNE
001A	7E XX XX	JMP, extnd, to monitor

Fig. 10-10. The assembled one-second delay program.

Loc	Code	Name
000E	86 36	LDAA, immed, 60
0010	CE D9 03	LDX, immed, 55555
0013	01	NOP
0014	01	NOP
0015	01	NOP
0016	01	NOP
0017	01	NOP
0018	09	DEX
0019	26 F8	BNE, to NOP
001B	01	NOP
001C	01	NOP
001D	4A	DECA
001E	26 F0	BNE, to LDX
0020	7E XX XX	JMP, to monitor

Fig. 10-15. The assembled one-minute loop program.

Loc	Code	Name
000C	C6 02	LDAB, immed, minutes
000E	86 3C	LDAA, immed, 60
0010	CE D9 03	LDX, immed, 55555
0013	01	NOP
0014	01	NOP
0015	01	NOP
0016	01	NOP
0017	01	NOP
0018	09	DEX
0019	26 F8	BNE, to NOP
001B	01	NOP
001C	01	NOP
001D	4A	DECA
001E	26 F0	BNE, to LDX
0020	5A	DECB
0021	26 EB	BNE, to LDAA
0023	7E XX XX	JMP, to monitor

Fig. 10-19. The assembled programmable timer program.

CHAPTER 11

Configuring an I/O Port

Using the 6800 involves a combination of software and hardware manipulation. Great I/O flexibility is available to the programmer who can, through software, configure the I/O hardware.

Objectives

You will be able to:

1. Sketch a block diagram of a 6820
2. Access the DDR and DR through the CR
3. Configure an input or output port

Most applications involve connecting the processor to one or more external devices. All parallel I/O signals, not RS 232 or a 20-mA loop, are routed through a special device called a peripheral interface adaptor (PIA). A block diagram of a PIA is shown in Fig. 11-1. Notice that the PIA is divided into two I/O ports. Since they are quite similar, port A will be discussed and the peculiarities of B mentioned.

An I/O port is external data's entrance to and exit from the processor. The port communicates with the processor via the data, address, and control buses. It communicates with the

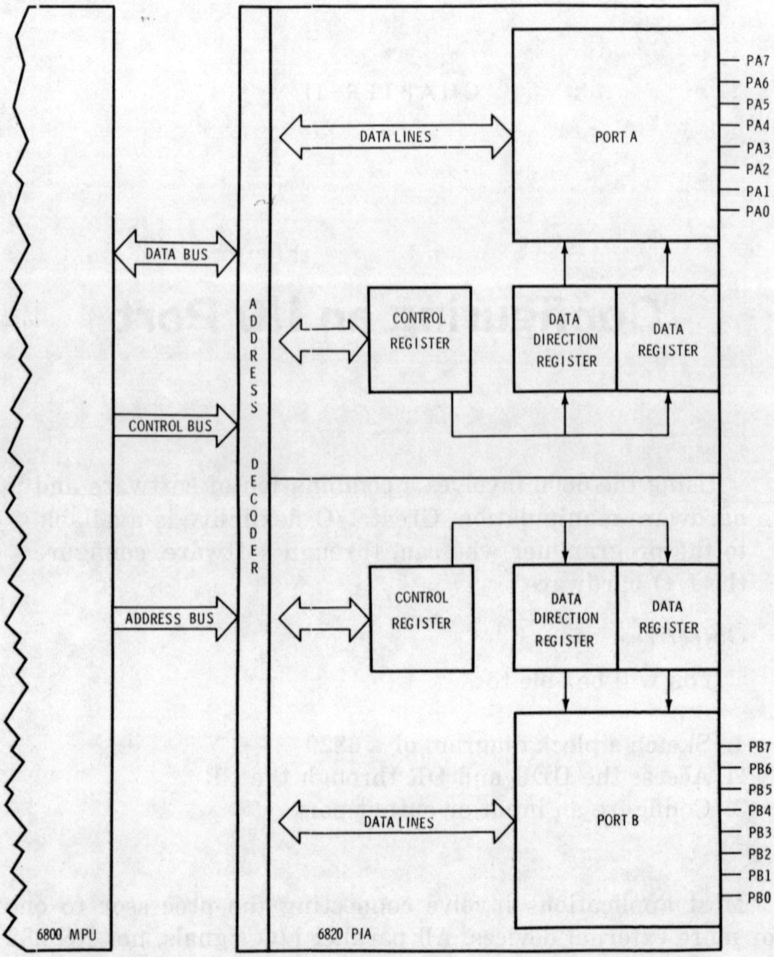

Fig. 11-1. A block diagram of a peripheral interface adapter.

outside world via eight lines, labeled PA0–PA7, that correspond to D0–D7 of the data bus. Lines PA0–PA7 are seen by the processor as a memory location.

Treating a group of eight I/O lines as a memory byte has several advantages. No special I/O instructions are needed, data on PA0–PA7 can participate directly in a program as a regular memory byte. Evaluation of external data can begin when it is placed on the I/O lines. Since I/O ports are seen as memory locations, thousands of ports, and through them I/O devices, can be connected directly to the processor.

Port A has been called an I/O port because it can serve as an input port, an output port, or a combination of both. Each line can be individually configured as either input or output. The port could have three input and five output lines, four input and four output lines, seven input and one output line, or any other I/O combination that would total eight. Being able to use the port as needed allows the programmer extreme flexibility.

The contents of the data direction register, located inside the 6820, determine the direction of data flow for each I/O line. Writing a one into a DDR bit sets the corresponding peripheral line as an output. Storing a zero in a DDR bit makes the corresponding line an input. Writing A6, 1010 0110, into the DDR would make PA0, PA3, PA4, and PA6 input lines and PA1, PA2, PA5, and PA7 output lines.

When a line is configured as an output, the output register latches or holds the output data and places it on the output lines. If the DDR contains FF, making all eight lines outputs, and the program generates 7E as output data, 7E is stored in the OR and simultaneously placed on the output lines. Output data, 7E, will remain on the output lines until new data replaces it in the OR.

The OR does not, however, store input data. Input data is read directly from the peripheral lines. Should data on an input line change before it can be read, the processor reads the new data. Should data on an input line change while being read, during an LDAX, the data actually read is questionable. Input data is usually stored in a regular memory location if it is not to be used immediately by the program.

The control register, CR, decodes the contents of the DDR and sets up the I/O lines. It is also vital in gaining access to the DDR or OR. Although the port has three addressable registers; the CR, DDR, and OR, it is assigned only two memory addresses. The location of these addresses is determined by the connection of five PIA lines, three Chip Selects, and two Register Selects, to address bus lines. Changing the PIA connections changes the addresses location. The register addresses are adjacent in memory.

One of the addresses is always the control register. The other address accesses either the DDR or the OR depending on the condition of bit two in the control register. If bit two of the CR is 0, the DDR will be accessed; if bit two of the CR is 1, the OR will be accessed. When a port is configured, bit two of the CR must be reset to access the DDR and the desired configuration stored in the DDR. Finally, bit two of the CR must be set to access the port which can then be used. Port A is configured in the flowchart of Fig. 11-2 and the program

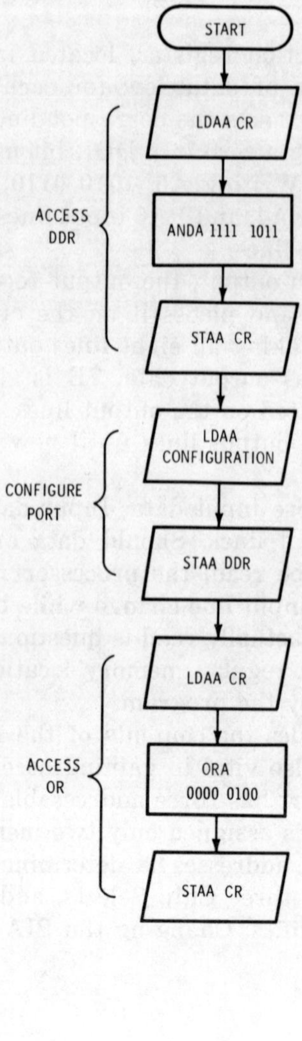

Fig. 11-2. A flowchart configuring port A.

of Fig. 11-3. Port A is at 8004 and 8005. The control register is 8005.

Notice that the ANDA and ORA instructions, used to select the DDR and OR, change only bit two of the control register. The other bits of the CR configure the interrupt lines, discussed in Chapter 13, and must not be disturbed when changing bit two. Enter and run the program of Fig. 11-1 substituting the proper PIA addresses for your system. Nothing observable should happen since the port is just initialized. Lines PA0–PA3 are output lines, and lines PA4 and PA7 are input lines.

Write and assemble in Fig. 11-4 a program that will make output line PA0 high and output lines PA1–PA3 low. Compare your program with the listing of Fig. 11-5 at the end of the chapter.

Loc	Code	Name
0058		

Fig. 11-4. Write a program controlling output lines.

Peripheral lines PA0–PA7 are usually brought to an edge connector or terminal block. Refer to the hardware manual of your system to determine the location of lines PA0–PA7. Carefully connect a dc voltmeter capable of reading 5 volts between PA0 and the system ground. Record the reading ______. Record the condition of PA1 ______. Run the program of Fig. 11-2. Record the condition of PA0 ______. Record the condition of PA1 ______. PA0 should go to a logical 1 and PA1 should remain low.

Modify the program of Fig. 11-2 to make PA0 low and PA1 high. Change the configuration word to 02. Run the modified program. Measure and record PA0 ______. Measure and record PA1 ______. PA0 should be low and PA1 should be high. Attempting to write data to PA4–PA7 is futile since those lines are configured as inputs.

Examine and record the contents of the control register ______ and the data direction register ______. Reset the system by pressing the reset button. Examine and record the contents of the CR ______ and DDR ______. Both should contain 00. One of the control lines connecting the 6820 to the 6800 is the reset line. Activating the reset on the PIA zeros all internal registers and all I/O lines become inputs. Resetting I/O lines as inputs prevents accidental starting of machinery connected to an I/O line when the system is powered up. The software of a system must, soon after reset, configure the I/O ports that it needs in the process it controls. A development or hobbyest system that uses a front panel or hex keyboard must configure the port needed to talk to them. Few differences exist between Ports A and B. Like A, port B is assigned two addresses that are adjacent to those of port A. It contains a CR,

Loc	Code	Name
0020		

Fig. 11-6. Write a program configuring port B.

DDR, and OR that function like their counterparts in port A. The two sets of identical registers are distinguished by adding A or B to abbreviations. Port A contains CRA, DDRA, and ORA; port B contains CRB, DDRB, and ORB. Port B has eight programmable I/O lines labeled PB0–PB7. Reading the contents of the output register differs for A and B. The state of an output line in port A will be read incorrectly if the load on that line pulls its 1 output, voltage below the TTL defined 2.4 volts, even though the attached load device is seeing a 1 on that line. Input lines will, of course, be read correctly. Port B does not exhibit this characteristic; the true status of an output line will always be read. Port A and B exhibit other differences that affect output drive and the operation of the interrupt lines. These will be discussed in Chapters 12 and 13.

Write and assemble in Fig. 11-6 a program that will configure port B as six input lines PB1–PB6 and two input lines PB0 and PB7. The program should make the output lines high, read the input lines, and store their contents at 0010.

Compare your program with Fig. 11-7 at the end of the chapter. Enter and run the program. Check PB1–PB6 for high outputs and examine and record the contents of 0010.

Proper connection of an external device to an I/O line is as important as the configuration of the line itself. Care must be taken to protect the processor system. Interfacing considerations will be discussed in Chapter 12.

Loc	Code	Name
0040	B6 80 05	LDAA, extnd, CR
0043	84 FB	ANDA, immed, 1111 1011
0045	B7 80 05	STAA, extnd, CR
0048	86 OF	LDAA, immed, config OF
004A	B7 80 04	STAA, extnd, DDR
004D	B6 80 05	LDAA, extnd, CR
0050	8A 04	ORA, immed, 0000 0100
0052	B7 80 05	STAA, extnd, CR
0055	7E XX XX	JMP, extnd, to monitor

Fig. 11-3. The assembled configuring port A program.

Loc	Code	Name
0058	86 01	LDAA, immed, 01
005A	B7 80 04	STAA, extnd, Port A
005D	7E XX XX	JMP, extnd, to monitor

Fig. 11-5. The assembled output controller program.

Loc	Code	Name
0020	B6 80 07	LDAA, extnd, CRB
	84 FB	ANDA, immed, 1111 1011
	B7 80 07	STAA, extnd, CRB
	86 7E	LDAA, immed, 7E
	B7 80 06	STAA, extnd, DDRB
	B6 80 07	LDAA, extnd, CRB
	8A 04	ORA, immed, 0000 0100
	B7 80 07	STAA, extnd, CRB
	86 7E	LDAA, immed, 7E
	B7 80 06	STAA, extnd, Port B outputs
	B6 80 06	LDAA, extnd, Port B
	97 10	STAA, direct, Port B inputs
	7E XX XX	JMP, extnd, to monitor

Fig. 11-7. The assembled port B configuration program.

CHAPTER 12

Interfacing

The programmable timer can be used with I/O lines in applications ranging from security systems to glass furnaces to refrigerator defrosters. External signals from these devices must be buffered or conditioned to match the drive and load capabilities of PIA I/O lines. Proper buffering, called interfacing, is a crucial consideration in any processor system.

Objectives

You will be able to:

1. List the drive and load characteristics of the 6820 peripheral lines
2. Determine the type of I/O buffering required by an external device
3. Use a relay as a buffer
4. Build a programmable controller

All I/O lines on the 6820 are TTL compatible. The TTL is a widely used IC logic family. Being TTL compatible means an output line must be 0.4 volt or less for a logic zero or 2.4 volts or greater for a logic one; an input line will accept 0.8 volt or less as a logic zero and 2.0 volts or more as a logic one. A standard TTL load is the ability to sink, or serve as ground for, 1.5 mA of current. Each I/O line on the PIA is capable of driving one TTL load or serving as one TTL load. Port B lines can, in addition, supply up to 1.0 mA of current at 1.5 volts. This is enough power to directly drive a transistor. Any device that cannot accept or deliver a TTL compatible signal must be buffered. Buffering can, in addition, electrically isolate the processor system from potentially destructive voltage and current spikes found in power control applications.

Not all devices require buffering. The clothes dryer control keyboard of Fig. 12-1 is a good example. Located on the top panel of the dryer, the keyboard allows the operator to select drying time and temperature and to start and stop the dryer. Buffering is not required since the keys just ground the PIA input lines. Probability of noise is small since the keyboard will be located close to the PIA. The resistors on the port B lines pull the input voltage to +5 when no key is depressed.

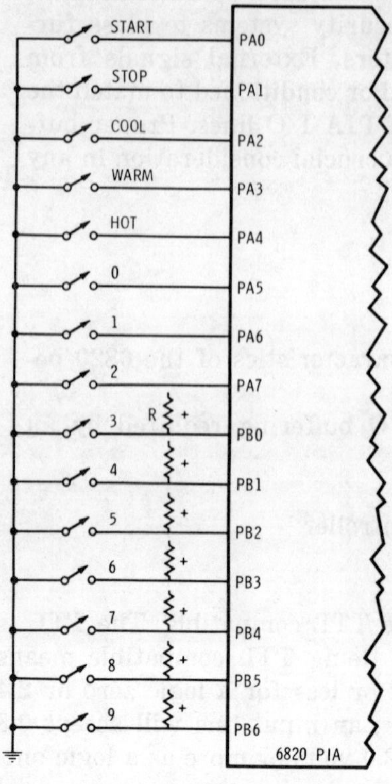

Fig. 12-1. A dryer keyboard.

The output circuit of a port B line, while providing increased output drive, needs the pull ups.

The monitor for this system configures all lines as inputs and scans the keyboard looking for a depression. When it senses a depression the monitor should wait about two milliseconds and examine the same key again. If the line is still low, the monitor can assume that an actual depression has occurred since most noise pulses do not last two milliseconds. The monitor will store that data, wait for another depression, and, when time and temperature has been entered, respond to a start depression.

The keys on this dryer can be rearranged to use fewer PIA lines as in Fig. 12-2.

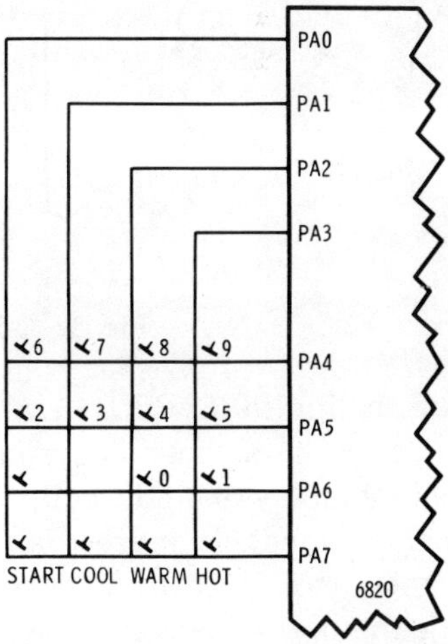

Fig. 12-2. A matrix keyboard.

The monitor configures PA0–PA3 as output and PA4–PA7 as inputs. It sets one output line high and examines the input lines for a depression. If one is not detected, each of the other output lines is individually set high and the inputs are examined. When a depression is detected, the key depressed can be identified by its row-column location. A large number of keys can be handled by a relatively small number of I/O lines by using this type of key matrix.

Cash registers, data terminals, microwave ovens, and soft drink machines all contain keyboards that are just as easily connected to the PIA. Many other processes feed the processor go no-go signals that can be similarly connected. Analog signals cannot, of course, be directly connected to the processor. Analog to digital (A/D) conversion is discussed in Chapter 14.

Most outputs require some buffering since the drive capability of an output line is relatively limited. Notable exceptions are transistors used to drive segments and digits in seven segment LED displays. The dryer keyboard developed should have a companion display to indicate drying time and temperature. A typical segment driver interface is shown in Fig. 12-3. Notice the base resistors limit the current into the

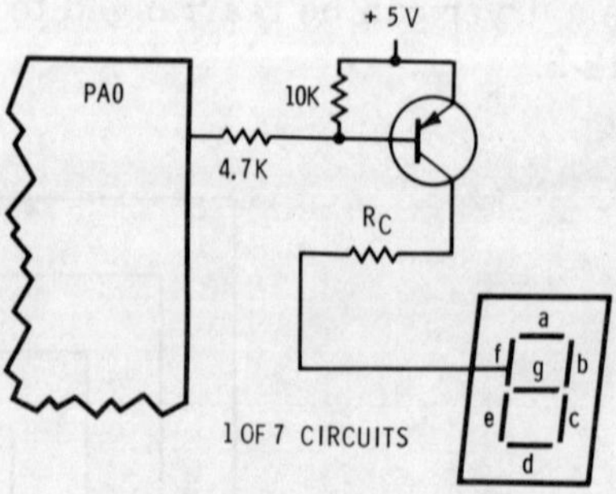

Fig. 12-3. Driving a display.

output line to less than 1 mA. The collector resistor is chosen to limit the segment current to its rated value. A seven segment display would require seven identical circuits, one for each segment. If more than one digit is desired a multiplexed display can be formed by providing digit drivers and connecting the digit-like segments together.

Some applications may require the processor to drive external TTL circuitry. The dryer's time display could be implemented as shown in Fig. 12-4. A PIA output register holds the drying time that is divided into two BCD characters, minutes and tens of minutes. When the dryer is started, the monitor enters a timing loop and decrements the output register after each minute. The BCD characters are fed to the 7447s and to the seven-segment decoder drivers that provide drive for the display. The inputs of the 7447s, however, act as more than one TTL load and cannot be directly driven by the PIA lines. The TTL hex inverters (7404s) can be placed between the PIA lines and the 7447s. Each inverter acts as one TTL load that can be driven by a PIA line and it can drive 10 TTL loads allowing it to drive the 7447 inputs.

The inverter also allows the monitor to be simplified. The DAA instruction, for BCD numbers, can be used only after addition instructions. The time display should be decremented after each elapsed minute. If the monitor inverts the time input from the keyboard before it is stored in the PIA output register, the proper time will be displayed since the 7404 in-

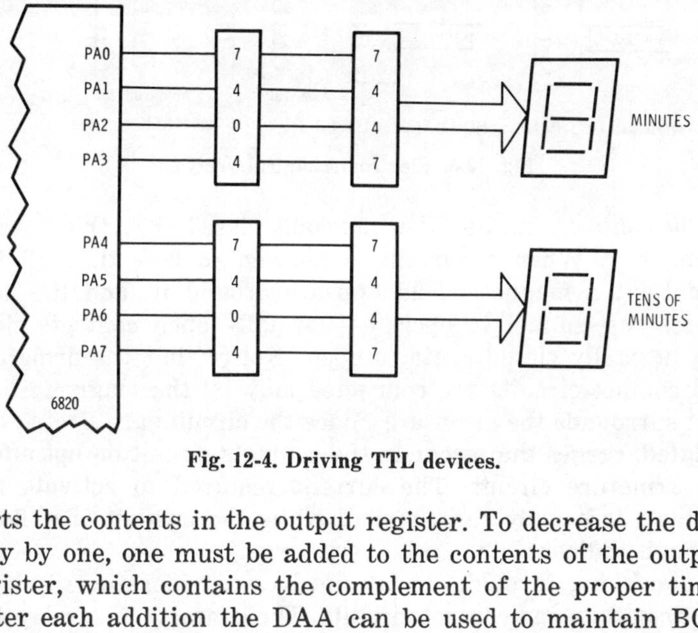

Fig. 12-4. Driving TTL devices.

verts the contents in the output register. To decrease the display by one, one must be added to the contents of the output register, which contains the complement of the proper time. After each addition the DAA can be used to maintain BCD output.

Although keyboard and display systems are popular they form just part of a total control system. Generally, the processor must be able to control devices that consume relatively large amounts of power. The dryer controller must be able to start and stop the motor and heating elements.

Power control increases the importance of interfacing. The interface must now protect the processor from deadly voltage and current surges that occur when power equipment is started or stopped. Protecting the processor means electrically isolating it from the system it is controlling. Isolation can be achieved by the use of relays or optical couplers.

Relays are electrically operated switches that allow a relatively small amount of power to control, turn on or off, a relatively large amount of power. Traditionally, a relay consists of a coil of wire, called the armature, that is placed close to a pair of contacts as shown in Fig. 12-5.

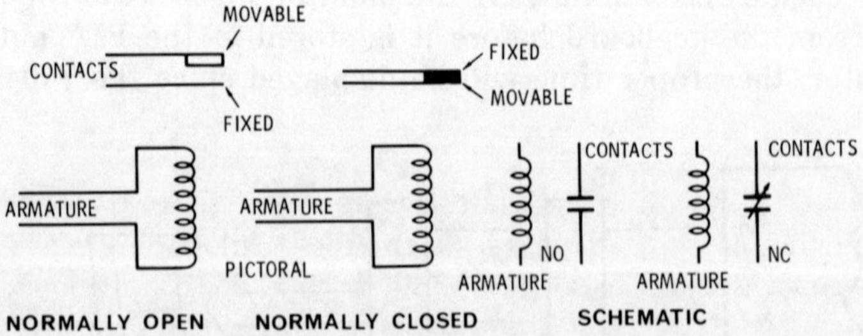

Fig. 12-5. Electromechanical relays.

The contacts can be either normally closed (nc) or normally open (no). When a current is allowed to flow through the armature, a magnetic field appears around it, and the field causes the contact to operate—normally open contacts close and normally closed contacts open. Notice that the armature and contact circuits are connected only by the magnetic field that surrounds the armature. Since the circuits are electrically isolated, surges that occur in the contacts circuit do not affect the armature circuit. The current required to activate the contacts is usually rather small while the current that flows through the contacts can be very large.

Interfacing through a relay involves considerations in both the armature and contact circuits. The contacts of a relay are rated according to the amount of voltage and current they can handle, it is important to use a relay that can handle the load. Relay specifications always include the amount of armature voltage required to activate the contacts. Either the required armature current or the armature resistance is also listed. The most desirable armature specifications would be 2.5 volts at less than 1 mA of current. Such a relay could be connected directly to a PIA output line. Recently a large variety of TTL compatible relays have become available. Unfortunately most of these relays are voltage compatible but represent more than one TTL load. Since a standard TTL gate can easily drive these relays they are often used as buffers as in Fig. 12-6. The

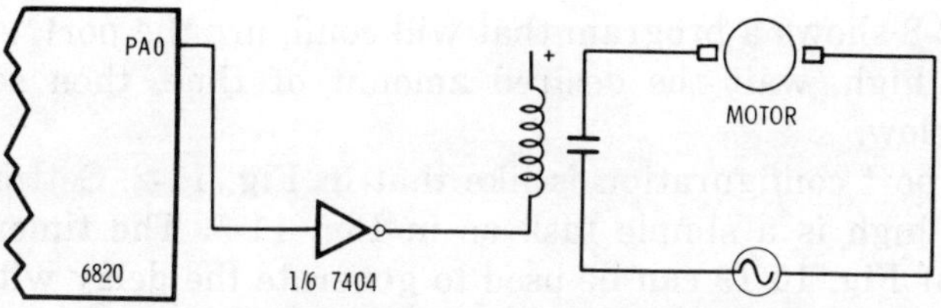

Fig. 12-6. Interfacing with a TTL compatible relay.

PA0 drives the 7404 which drives the relay which controls the motor. One 7404 could drive as many as six relays.

Not all relays are TTL compatible. Twelve-volt relays have been widely used for years so are plentiful and inexpensive. Driving a 12-volt relay is simple with a TTL open collector buffer/driver. The 7406 and 7416 are open collector inverter buffers that can sink 30 or 40 mA of current and can handle 15 or 30 volts. The 7407 and 7417 are open collector buffers that have voltage and current specifications equal to the 7406 and 7416. An open collector buffer has the collector of the output transistor disconnected. A discrete resistor must connect it to the positive supply. The opportunity to choose a resistor that will limit the current to the desired value and the high voltage and current specifications make the buffers ideal for driving relays. Fig. 12-7 shows a 7407 driving a 12-volt, 40-mA relay that has an armature resistance of 300 ohms. Discrete transistors can also be used to drive relays in the same configuration used to drive LEDs in Fig. 12-4. It may, occasionally, be necessary to drive a relay with a power transistor that must be driven with a TTL buffer.

The timer in Chapter 10 can be combined with the port configuration of Chapter 11 and the interfacing of Chapter 12 to form a practical programmable controller. The flowchart of

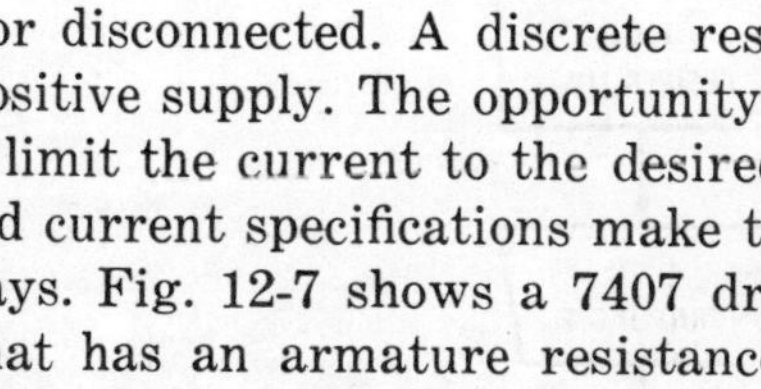

Fig. 12-7. Driving a 12-volt relay.

Fig. 12-8 shows a program that will configure the port, set the output high, wait the desired amount of time, then set the output low.

The port configuration is like that in Fig. 11-2. Setting the output high is a simple task as in Fig. 11-5. The timer program of Fig. 10-19 can be used to generate the delay with one

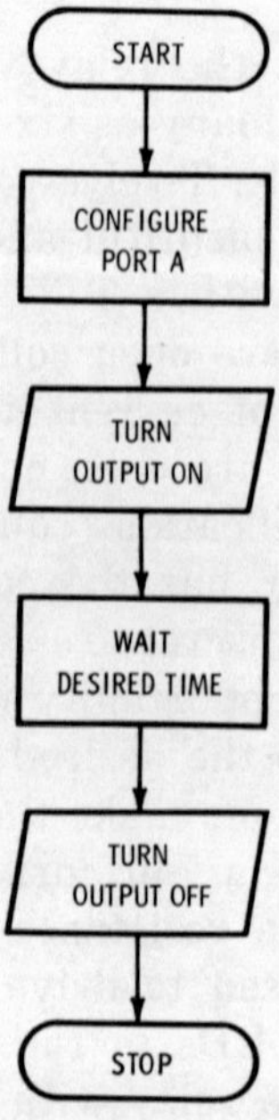

Fig. 12-8. A programmable controller flowchart.

modification. It would be easier to load the desired delay into 000A, go to 000B, and press go to start the program. The LDAB will have to load B with the contents of 000A, a change of addressing mode. Write and assemble in Fig. 12-9 (next page) the programmable controller of Fig. 12-8. Write the program to configure PA2 as an output and PA0, PA1, and PA3–PA7 as inputs. Compare your program with the listing of Fig. 12-10 at the end of the chapter.

Obtain a 5-, 6-, or 12-volt relay and carefully interface it to PA2. *Caution!* The 6820 and all other 6800 family devices are extremely sensitive to static discharge from external objects. *Never* attempt to connect or disconnect an external device when the 6800 system is powered up. *Always* remove

Loc	Code	Name
000A		

cont on next page

Fig. 12-9. Writing the programmable controller program in Fig. 12-8.

power. *Always* ground yourself and any tools through a one-megohm resistor before connecting or disconnecting any devices. *Caution!* Do not turn the processor on. Connect a table lamp to the relay contacts as shown in Fig. 12-11.

Notice that the relay contacts are in the "hot" side of the ac line. Before you enter and run your program consider the action of the relay. To meter your program you must turn on and reset the processor. When the processor is reset, the control register and data direction register of the 6820 are reset, making all peripheral lines inputs. A TTL interface will see that input as a one and, if it is a noninverting buffer, make its output high activating the relay. This could be a dangerous condition if the relay load was a machine. A TTL interface should be an inverting buffer (such as the 7406). A zero must be written to PA2 to activate the relay since the 7406 will invert it and activate the relay. The interface circuit deter-

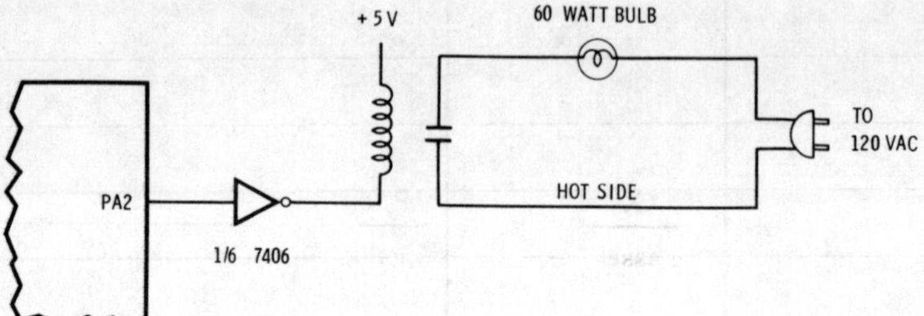

Fig. 12-11. Controlling a lamp.

mines whether a one or zero activates the relay. Care should be taken to prevent accidental turn on.

With the discussion of interfacing, a multitude of applications are available. Little hardware is required for the processor to control everything from a coffee pot to a darkroom light to a burglar alarm to a commercial french fryer. With one 6820 you can control all of these devices.

Loc	Code	Name
000A		Desired "on" time
000B	B6 80 05	LDAA, extnd, CR
000E	84 FB	ANDA, immed, 1111 1011
0010	B7 80 05	STAA, extnd, CR
0013	86 04	LDAA, immed, configuration
0015	B7 80 04	STAA, extnd, DDR
0018	B6 80 05	LDAA, extnd, CR
001B	8A 04	ORA, immed, 0000 0100
001D	B7 80 05	STAA, extnd, CR
0020	86 00	LDAA, immed
0022	B7 80 04	STAA, extnd, OR turn on device
0025	D6 0A	LDAB, direct, minutes
0027	86 3C	LDAA, immed, 60
0029	CE D9 03	LDX, immed, 55555
002C	01	NOP
002D	01	NOP
002E	01	NOP
002F	01	NOP
0030	01	NOP
0031	09	DEX
0032	26 F8	BNE, to NOP
0034	01	NOP
0035	01	NOP
0036	4A	DECA
0037	26 F0	BNE, to LDX
0039	5A	DECB
003A	26 EB	BNE, to LDAA
003C	86 04	LDAA, immed, 00
003E	B7 80 04	STAA, extnd, OR turn off device
0041	7E XX XX	JMP, extnd, to monitor

Fig. 12-10. The assembled programmable controller program.

CHAPTER 13

Interrupts

The speed and power of a microprocessor allow it to be responsible for many tasks at the same time, especially if the tasks are performed infrequently or irregularly. Interrupts give the processor great flexibility in handling more than one task.

Objectives

You will be able to:

1. List the processor's responses to an interrupt, NMI or IRQ
2. Explain use of the stack
3. Configure CA1, CA2, CB1, and CB2 as I/O lines or interrupts
4. Explain software polling of multiple interrupts
5. Write an interrupt program
6. Use subroutines

A processor might be responsible for a fire alarm, security system, heating system, and be available for game playing or supervision of an automatic bottling machine. If the processor's operating system constantly examines each alarm and heating sensor for activity, the processor will have very little time left to control another process or play games. All of the time the processor spends checking the sensors is wasted if they do not require service. A fire and security system should, hopefully, never be used, and the heating system should require only sporadic attention.

A much more efficient system in terms of the processor's time would allow it to ignore the alarm and heating systems until they ask for attention. Such a service system, when needed, would free most of the processor's time for other tasks. Service on demand is possible with the 6800 using the interrupt inputs. Two interrupt lines are provided to allow connection of devices needing infrequent service.

A system that utilizes interrupts normally runs a control, monitor, or other master program. An interrupt request occurs during the execution of the master program. Before it deals with the interrupting device, the processor finishes execution of the current instruction. It then stores the contents of its vital registers in a special area of memory called the stack. By saving the vital registers the processor can resume execution of the master program when it has finished servicing the interrupting device. The vital registers are the program counter, the index register, the accumulators, and the condition code register.

The stack is just an area in read-write memory that is reserved for the registers' contents during an interrupt. Its location in memory is arbitrary and is chosen by the programmer. Just as the processor uses the program counter to hold the location of the next instruction, it uses the stack pointer to hold the next available stack location. The stack pointer, SP, is a 16-bit register contained inside of the 6800. The location of the stack is determined by the stack pointer, which can be loaded from or stored in memory, LDS, STS; incremented or decremented, INS, DES; or transferred to or from the index register, TSX, TXS. The stack must be initialized before an interrupt occurs. It can be initialized by loading the chosen starting location into the stack pointer. It is usually initialized at the beginning of the program. The stack is a last in first out area in which data is stored in successively lower memory locations. If SP is initialized at 0100 and an interrupt occurs, PCL is stored at 0100, PCH at 00FF, Index Register Low at 00FE, Index Register High at 00FD, ACCA at 00FC, ACCB at 00FB, and CR at 00FA. After each byte is stored the SP is decremented one; after the CCR is stored the SP contains 00F9, the next available stack location. The processor, upon receipt of an interrupt, automatically stores the registers on the stack; no action is needed by the program.

After finishing the current instruction and storing the registers, the processor is ready to begin servicing the interrupt. Before it can execute a service program, the processor must be pointed to the location of its first instruction. Just as the processor looks at the highest two bytes in memory to find the reset vector, it looks at the next highest bytes, called the interrupt vector, to find the location of the first instruction in the interrupt service program. The interrupt vector is, like the reset vector, usually stored in ROM. The interrupt vector is jammed into the program counter, and the next instruction executed is the first instruction in the service program.

When the service program is completed, the processor should resume execution of the master program at the point of interruption. To continue execution, the stack contents must be reloaded into the processor's registers. One instruction, the Return from Interrupt (RTI), restores the registers to their former states and execution of the master resumes. The RTI must always be the last instruction in an interrupt service program.

Two levels of interrupt capability are provided on the 6800. Both levels are TTL compatible. One, the Interrupt Request (IRQ) line, allows great flexibility in handling multiple interrupts. It is activated when pulled low. The security, fire, and heating systems mentioned earlier could all be handled using the IRQ. Inputs from all three systems would be connected together, wire or'd, and connected to the IRQ input with a pull up resistor. Any of the three systems could activate the IRQ by pulling it low. Since several devices may be connected to the IRQ, the processor takes measures to allow it to completely service one interrupt at a time.

The condition code register's bit 4 is the interrupt mask flag I. When the I flag is set (1), the processor will not recognize an interrupt from the IRQ line. When it is reset (0), the processor will recognize an interrupt from the IRQ line. The processor automatically sets the I flag when it recognizes an interrupt. The IRQ vector is then fetched from its memory location and the service program executed.

When it determines which device is asking for service, the processor must tell that device that it is being serviced and should let the IRQ line go inactive (high). Notifying the device of its service is called clearing the interrupt. The interrupt can be cleared either at the beginning or end of a service program.

Sometimes it is desirable to allow an interrupt service program to be interrupted. If this is desirable, the interrupt should be cleared at the beginning of the service program. Although the interrupt has been cleared and the IRQ line is high, the processor will not recognize another interrupt until the I flag is reset. The Clear Interrupt Mask (CLI) instruction can be used to reset the I flag. The I flag should not, however, be reset until the interrupt has been cleared. Resetting the I flag first will cause the processor to recognize the same interrupt again, and this an undesirable situation.

Clearing and resetting an interrupt early in the service program allows another device to ask for service by interrupting. If this occurs, execution of the first service program will be stopped and its registers stored on the stack. The second interrupt will be serviced and then the first interrupt's registers will be pulled from the stack and execution of its service program will continue. After the first interrupt has been serviced, the master program will be resumed. Any number of interrupt service programs can be interrupted, called nesting, so long as the stack has enough memory locations. The stack should be initialized in an area that will not conflict with program or data memory.

Some systems may work more efficiently if one interrupt is completely serviced before the processor is allowed to recognize another. This can be accomplished by waiting to clear the interrupt and reset the I flag until the end of the service program, just before the RTI.

Occasionally a program or section of a program is critical to the system's operation and must not be disturbed by an interrupt. The Set Interrupt Mask (SEI) instruction can be used to set the I flag and prevent recognition of an interrupt. At the end of the critical section the CLI can be used to allow recognition of interrupts.

Different service possibilities exist with the nonmaskable interrupt (NMI) line. As its name implies the NMI cannot be ignored by the processor—it is not affected by the I flag. When the NMI is activated, by the negative going edge of the request signal, the processor must service it. An NMI request is serviced like an IRQ; the current instruction is finished; the internal registers are pushed onto the stack; the I flag is set; and the NMI vector is fetched. The NMI vector is separate from the IRQ vector, as shown in Fig. 13-1.

Location	Vector
FFFF FFFE	Reset Vector
FFFD FFFC	NMI Vector
FFFB FFFA	SWI Vector
FFF9 FFF8	IRQ Vector

Fig. 13-1. Vector locations.

The reset vector, as previously stated, resides at the two highest locations. The NMI vector is just below it, followed by the SWI vector (yet to be discussed) and the IRQ vector. Although the vectors are shown from FFF8 to FFFF they do not have to rest there. Few processor systems will contain 65,536 memory bytes but all systems must use the vectors. When the reset vector is fetched the processor makes all address lines high, indicating FFFF. If a system does not use all 16 address lines to access memory the actual address located will be lower than FFFF. A designer must, then, take care to have the vectors at the locations because the processor will look for them.

Separate interrupt vectors accommodate different interrupt needs. NMI interrupts are reserved for devices that must have immediate service. Some measurement and data devices can only hold data valid for a short period of time and, therefore, need the immediate service provided through the NMI. Catastrophe indicators, such as fire detectors or power failure sensors, would, of course, be connected to the NMI line. Any number of devices can be wire or'd to the NMI. Only a reset has priority over the NMI input.

Since all parallel I/O signals are handled through the 6820 peripheral interface adaptor, the interrupt signals also pass

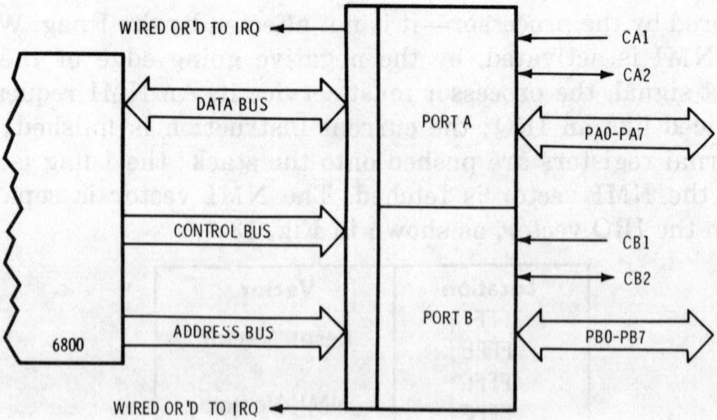

Fig. 13-2. The complete ports.

through the PIA. Each I/O port has two interrupt lines associated with it. They are designated in Fig. 13-2 as CA1, CA2, CB1, and CB2. Great flexibility is provided in the use of these lines.

Since CA1 and CB1 are identical, only CA1 will be discussed, but the discussion also applies to CB1. Interrupt line CA1 can be made sensitive to either a rising or falling edge and it can be allowed to or prohibited from activating the processor's IRQ line. Its mode of operation is controlled by the condition of bits 0 and 1 in the PIA's control register A (CRA). Fig. 13-3 shows the four possible modes.

CA1 can respond to either a rising or falling edge depending on bit 1; 0 represents a falling edge and 1 a rising edge. When the proper transition is made, the port notes the transition by setting bit 7 in the CRA. The condition of bit 0 determines whether the transition will cause the processor's IRQ line to be activated. In either case bit 7 is always set by a proper transition. When bit 0 is set and a proper transition occurs both bit 7 is set and the IRQ line is activated. By writ-

CRA bit No. 1	0	CA1 transition	IRQ line
0	0	falling edge	not affected
0	1	falling edge	activated on transition
1	0	rising edge	not affected
1	1	rising edge	activated on transition

Fig. 13-3. Configuring CA1.

ing the proper code words into ports' control registers, the processor can selectively ignore interrupt requests.

The flowchart of Fig. 13-4 demonstrates the configuration of CA1 as an interrupt that will respond to the falling edge of an input signal.

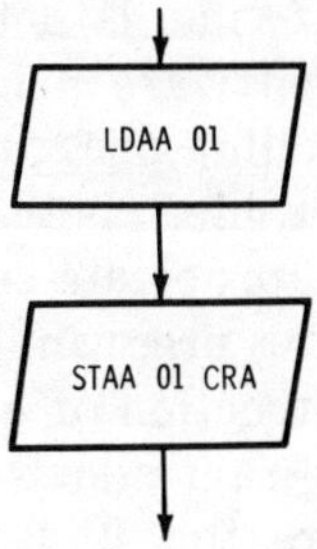

Fig. 13-4. A flowchart configuring CA1 as an interrupt.

The processor can choose to ignore an interrupt from this port by resetting bit 0 as shown in Fig. 13-5. The interrupt and bit 7 are reset when the processor reads the contents of output register A (ORA).

The importance of bit 7 can now be understood. A system may have none, one, or more than one interrupting device. When more than one device is capable of causing an interrupt, the processor must be able to determine which device needs

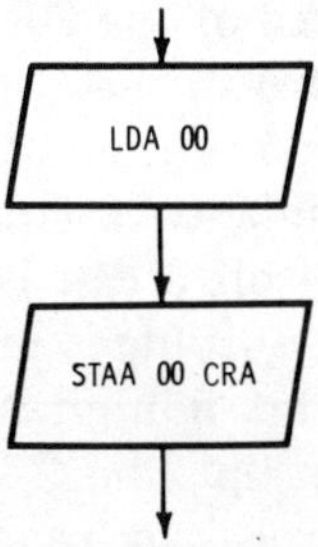

Fig. 13-5. A flowchart ignoring CA1.

service. Each device has its own interrupt service program. The processor should certainly respond differently to interrupt requests from the security and heating systems. By examining bit 7 of the control register of each port the processor can easily determine which device needs service. Such a program is called a polling program and is pointed to by the IRQ vector. When the polling program determines which device is requesting service it, then, jumps to the appropriate service routine. If two devices should request service at the same time the processor must know which has priority and which should be serviced first. Prioritizing interrupts can be done with discrete hardware or it can be made part of the interrupt polling program. If time is not critical and the interrupting devices can wait, software prioritizing is easier and less expensive. A simple polling program is shown in Fig. 13-6. The CA1 flag of each port, bit 7, is tested; and if it is set, the processor executes the appropriate service program.

The polling program is pointed to by the IRQ vector and by the last instruction of each service program. Returning to the polling program allows the processor to test for other interrupts before the RTI is performed. The interrupts can be prioritized by polling the ports in their order of importance.

Port A's other interrupt line is CA2, Port B's other interrupt line is CB2. Since CA2 and CB2 are similar only differences will be noted. Three bits in the port's control register, bits 3, 4, and 5, configure CA2. When bit 5 is zero, bits 3 and 4 can configure CA2 as an interrupt input on the processor's IRQ line. Fig. 13-7 shows the interrupt possibilities. Notice that bits 3 and 4 act like bits 0 and 1 for CA1.

Bit 6 of the CRA is CA2's I flag and is set any time a proper transition occurs. Bit 6 is reset when ORA is read by the processor. If bit 3 of the CRA is set and a proper transition occurs on CA2, bit 6 in the CRA is set and the IRQ line is activated.

When bit 5 in the CRA is set CA2 becomes an output. If bit 4 is also high, CA2 simply assumes the state of bit 3 in the CRA. Since bit 3 can be made high or low by writing into it CA2, as an output, is under program control.

Making bit 5 high and bit 3 high allows another output mode. Interrupt line CA2 is normally high in this mode. Each time the processor reads the port's input pins CA2 is taken low for one clock cycle. This output pulse can signal an external device that the processor has read its data. The device, perhaps an A/D converter, can then ready new data. Port B's CA2 operation in this condition differs slightly. Interrupt line CB2 is taken low each time the processor writes data to the output register. This pulse can be used to signal an external device that the processor has made new data available.

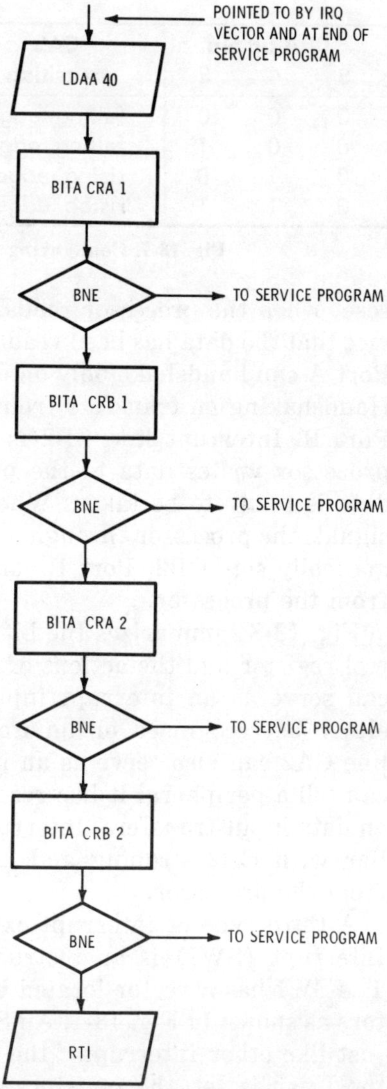

Fig. 13-6. A software polling flowchart.

Handshaking is the controlled exchange of data between two devices. Simple handshaking can be accomplished by setting CRA bit 5 high and bits 3 and 4 low. In this mode the peripheral device signals the processor that it has data ready by interrupting through CA1. Interrupt line CA2 is set high when the interrupt occurs telling the peripheral device to hold the data while it is read. Interrupt line CA2 is automatically

CRA bit No. 5	4	3	CA2 transition	IRQ line
0	0	0	falling edge	not affected
0	0	1	falling edge	activated on transition
0	1	0	rising edge	not affected
0	1	1	rising edge	activated on transition

Fig. 13-7. Configuring CA2 as an interrupt.

reset when the processor reads the input lines, telling the device that the data has been read and new data can be presented. Port A can handshake only on data transfers to the processor. Handshaking on transfers from the processor is possible with Port B. Interrupt line CB2 is automatically reset when the processor writes data to the port telling the peripheral that data is ready to be taken. When the device takes the data it signals the processor through an interrupt on CB1 which automatically sets CB2. Port B can handshake only on transfers from the processor.

Fig. 13-8 summarizes the bit assignments of the PIA's control register and the actions of CA1 and CA2. Generally, CA1 can serve as an interrupt input by setting bit 7 which can either be recognized or ignored by the processor. Interrupt line CA2 can also serve as an interrupt by setting bit 6, or it can tell a peripheral it has received data, or it can handshake on data input transfers. Interrupt lines CB1 and CB2 are similar with CB2 strobing and handshaking on data transfers from the processor.

A third type of interrupt exists in the 6800. The Software Interrupt (SWI) is an instruction that causes an interrupt. The SWI has a vector located between the IRQ and NMI vectors as shown in Fig. 13-1. An SWI is handled by the processor just like other interrupts; the current instruction is finished, the I flag is set, the registers are pushed onto the stack, and the SWI vector is fetched. The SWI vector must contain the address of the first instruction in the SWI service program. When the SWIs are placed after branch instructions or other critical points in a program, the internal registers are pushed onto the stack and can be examined to verify correct operation of the program. Called breakpoints, the SWIs are very helpful in debugging programs. An SWI service program may

		CA2 CONTROL				CA1 Control	
7	6	5	4	3	2	1	0
CA1 interrupt flag	CA2 interrupt flag	0 = CA2 interrupt 1 = CA2 output	If 5 = 0 same as bits 0 & 1, if 5 = 1: 1 CA2 follows bit 3 0 / output pulse on data read 0 / handshake on read	(If 5 = 1:) 1 / (output pulse on data read) 1 (handshake on read) 0	0 = DDR 1 = DR of port	0 = edge 1 = edge	0 = disables CA1 on IRQ 1 = enables CA1 on IRQ

Fig. 13-8. A summary of the CRA bits.

be as simple as a jump to monitor that allows the programmer to observe the stack contents.

A processor may need data about the process being controlled to continue execution of the control program. The data needed may be concerned with some parameter in the process being controlled. If the data is not ready when the processor needs it the processor must wait until it becomes available. The Wait (WAI) instruction simplifies the waiting process. When the processor encounters a WAI it prepares for an interrupt by pushing the internal registers onto the stack and then waiting for an interrupt to signal the availability of the data needed. The processor will resume activity on a reset, NMI, or IRQ if the I flag is not set. When the I flag is set only the reset or NMI will cause activity.

Besides storage of the registers, the stack is used in the execution of subroutines. A subroutine is a group of instructions that are frequently used in a program; they are coded only once and are easily accessible by the program. Any group of instructions can be designated a subroutine. Subroutines are usually placed after the main body of a program.

In a microprocessor monitor program the section of the program that generates a delay for keyboard inputs and display outputs may be used a dozen times in one pass through the monitor. Rather than coding the delay loop 12 times, the delay routine could be coded once and designated a subroutine. When the delay is needed in the program the programmer indicates that it is in a subroutine with either a Jump to Subroutine (JSR) or Branch to Subroutine (BSR) instruction. The extended address of the subroutine's first instruction follows the JSR, and the necessary offset follows the BSR.

When it encounters a JSR or BSR, the processor pushes the program counter onto the stack then begins execution of the subroutine at the specified location. At the end of the subroutine, the Return from Subroutine (RTS) instruction can be used to resume execution of the main program. The RTS, which is the last instruction of any subroutine, pulls the program counter from the stack and allows the main program to continue. Fig. 13-9 illustrates a simple subroutine.

Although a delay program would need no data from the main program, many conversion or math subroutines will work on data contained or generated in the main program. The pro-

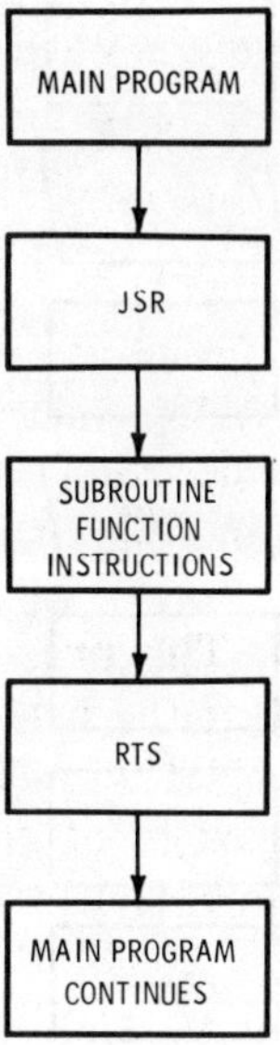

Fig. 13-9. A flowchart using a simple subroutine.

grammer can use the stack to pass information to and from the subroutinc. Data can be transferred to the subroutine by pushing it onto the stack with the Push Data onto Stack (PSHX) from accumulator instruction. The data must, of course, be loaded into an accumulator before the PSHX is used. Any number of bytes can be pushed onto the stack to be transferred to the subroutine. After execution of the JSR, the subroutine must pull the data passed to it from the stack. The Pull Data From Stack (PULX) pulls the last byte of data from the stack and loads it into the accumulator. The last two bytes on the stack are the program counter contents that are pushed by the JSR and point to the main program. The first two bytes pulled must be stored in memory and later replaced on the stack before the RTS. The subroutine can then pull the information passed to it from the stack. Near the end of the subroutine, before the RTS, the calculated data can be pushed onto the stack for transfer to the main program. Just before the RTS the program counter, pulled and stored at the beginning of the subroutine, must be pushed back onto the stack for transfer to the main program. Just before the RTS the program counter, pulled and stored at the beginning of the subroutine, must be pushed back onto the stack. Finally the

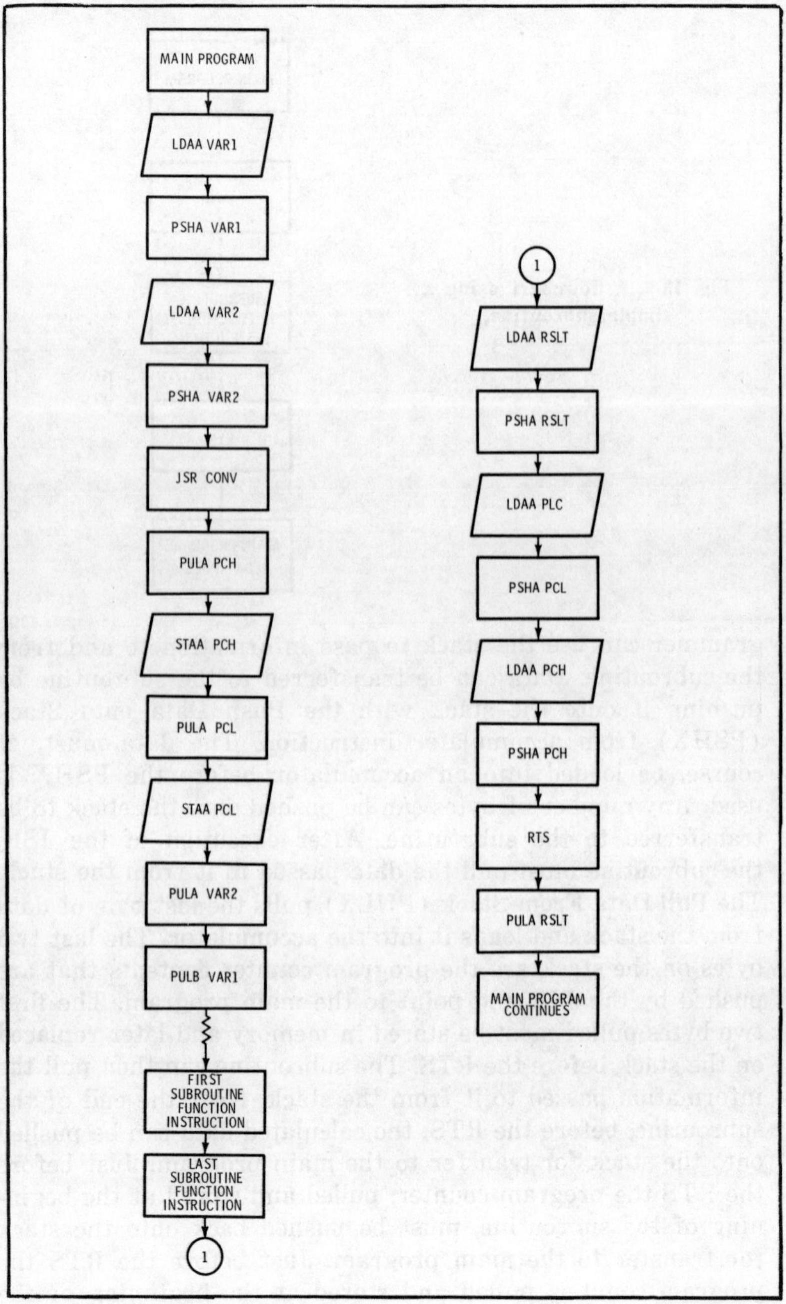

Fig. 13-10. This flowchart is passing data to and from a subroutine.

RTS can be executed. In the flowchart of Fig. 13-10 two bytes of data, VAR1 and VAR2, are passed to the subroutine and the result (RSLT) is passed back to the main program. After execution of the RTS, the result is pulled from the stack and the main program continues.

As Fig. 13-10 demonstrates, the use of a subroutine may require several bytes of program memory. Careful consideration should be given to the length and frequency of use of a routine before it is designated a subroutine. Prudently used, subroutines save program memory and programmer time.

Interrupts and subroutines are both powerful programming tools; they can save processor time and memory space. The use of interrupts and subroutines should be considered in almost all applications even though they may, upon consideration, not be used.

CHAPTER 14

D/A and A/D Conversion

Analog to digital (A/D) and digital to analog (D/A) converters are essential components of many industrial control systems. Although A/D and D/A converters have traditionally been expensive, the advent of the microprocessor and advances in IC technology allow these conversions to be done inexpensively and with a minimum of hardware.

Objectives

You will be able to:

1. Use an integrated D/A converter
2. Use a software-based successive approximation A/D converter

A digital to analog converter is a relatively simple device. Given a parallel digital word it produces an analog signal of proportionate size. Since each digital bit in a word is twice the size of the previous one most converters consist of a series of resistors, called a resistor ladder. Each resistor is half the size of the previous one so it produces twice the current. The resistor ladder is usually supported by a series of transistors that stabilize the current.

Eight- and ten-bit integrated D/As are readily available for less than 10 dollars in single quantities. These devices require a split, plus and minus, power supply that can be derived in many systems from the memory device power supplies. An external precision analog reference is not needed since it is included on the chip. Interfacing these devices is a simple task. A PIA port must, of course, be configured as an output port. Most D/As are TTL compatible so they can be directly connected to the output lines of the port or its TTL buffers. An analog signal is produced each time the processor writes to the port. Since the output register of the port latches the output word, the output of the converter constantly reflects the output register. The output of the converter may need to be buffered to protect it from analog spikes. Some converters produce an output current, others produce an output voltage. An output current can be easily converted to a voltage with an op amp. The output voltage is OV to $+V_{cc}$ (5v). An inexpensive D/A is interfaced to a port in Fig. 14-1.

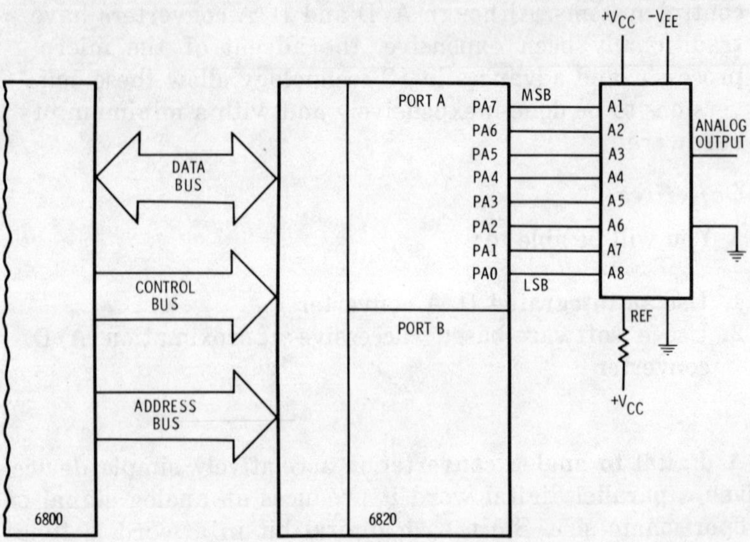

Fig. 14-1. Interfacing a D/A converter.

Software analog to digital conversion can be accomplished several ways but all are somewhat similar. Generally the processor guesses, through some algorithm, the value of the analog input. This guess is fed through an output port to a D/A converter whose output is compared with the analog input. Based on the comparison the processor either tries a new guess or discovers that its guess was correct and ends the conversion. The basic hardware used in all A/D schemes is shown in Fig. 14-2. The PBO is configured as an input. Differences in schemes are primarily differences in the algorithm used to develop the guess of the processor.

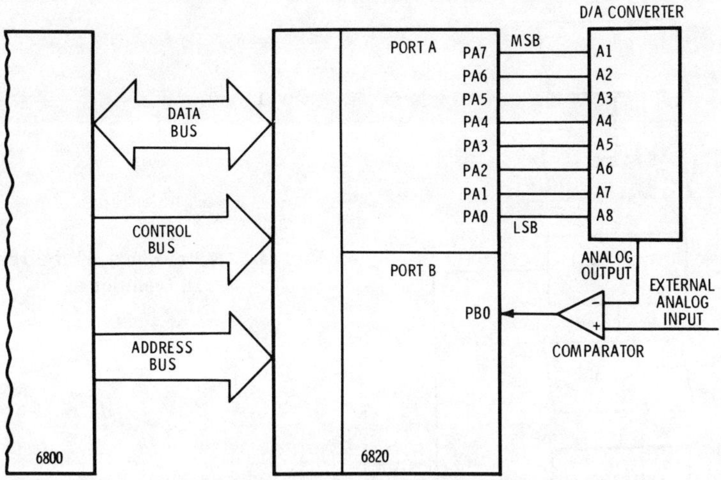

Fig. 14-2. A/D hardware requirements.

A very simple A/D conversion technique is the increasing ramp. The first guess of the processor is zero and each successive guess is one higher than the last. After each guess the output of the comparator is sampled. Thus, the guess of the processor gradually increases until it is equal to the analog input. The ramp technique is shown in the flowchart of Fig. 14-3.

Although the ramp technique is simple it can also be very slow, especially for relatively large external analog inputs. If time is not critical, it is an acceptable A/D technique.

Analog to digital by successive approximation is faster and more popular than the ramp technique. Instead of starting at zero and gradually increasing its guess, the processor first sets PA7, the most significant bit, high. If the comparison shows the guess too low, the MSB remains high and PA6 is set. If the original guess is too high, PA7 is reset and PA6 is set. Based on the next comparison, PA6 remains set or is reset.

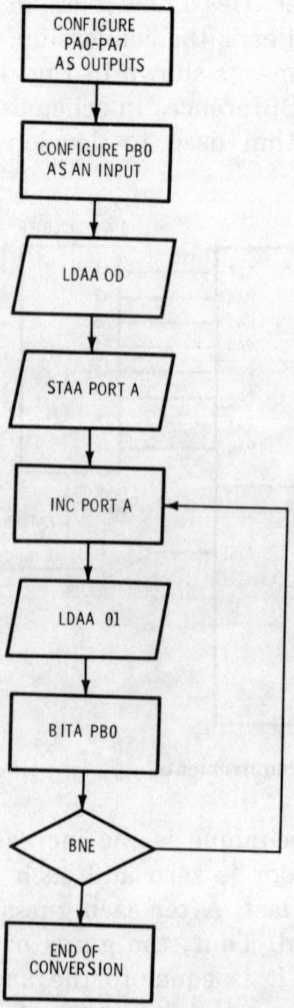

Fig. 14-3. A flowchart of the ramp A/D technique.

Each lower bit is set in turn and based on the comparison that follows is set or is reset. After all eight output lines have been tried, the conversion is complete and the correct digital word rests in the output register of the port. The successive approximation technique is shown in the flowchart of Fig. 14-4.

Accumulator B is used to count the number of bits tested in port A. One is successively placed in each bit position without disturbing the others by a rotating OR instruction operating in the immediate mode. After each pass the mask is rotated one position right. When each bit is set, Port B is read for the

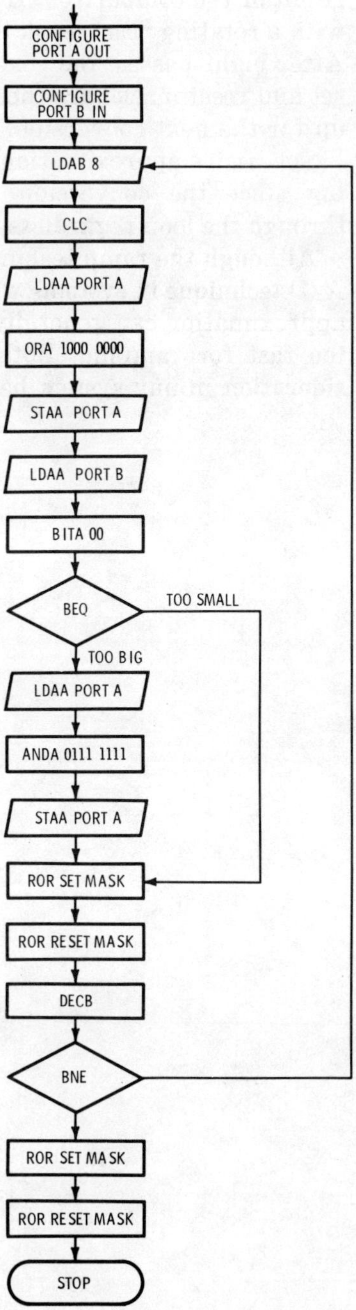

Fig. 14-4. A flowchart of A/D conversion by successive approximation.

result of the comparison. If the bit should be reset it is ANDed with a rotating reset mask that affects only the bit in question. After eight passes, the correct digital code is in Port A. The set and reset masks are then rotated one last time to set them up for the next conversion.

Successive approximation is usually much faster than ramping since the conversion is accomplished in eight passes through the loop regardless of the size of the analog input.

Although the ramp technique is very slow it is an acceptable A/D technique in systems where time is not critical. Successive approximation can generally be used in those systems that are too fast for ramping. Both techniques should be given consideration in any system because of their very low cost.

CHAPTER 15

System Design

Microprocessors are appearing in many new products. Use of a processor in a control system may or may not be advantageous. Unfortunately, no hard and fast rules exist for processor usage. Each control system and its parameters must be carefully examined before a decision can be made. The guidelines that follow are general and can be used for a wide variety of product applications or projects.

Objectives

You will be able to:

1. Determine if a processor is suitable for an application
2. Determine the hardware/software distribution in a system
3. Design software efficiently

Regardless of other considerations, a processor must meet the speed requirements of a system. A micro that can run as fast as Schottky TTL does not exist, the fastest 6800 product runs at 2 MHz. Although time is not critical in some systems, many processors have to deal with very fast peripherals or become part of peripherals that must be very fast. A processor controlled cash register should not hold up or slow down a master controller minicomputor that it may be feeding. Before any other factors are considered, the speed question should be resolved.

If a processor meets the speed demands of a system, the decision becomes economic. The simplest economic factor is that of parts costs. A very simple processor may be able to replace 50 or more discrete ICs at a lower cost. Video games provide a good example here. Early games, although quite simple, were made with many discrete TTL chips. Modern designs reduce the IC part count by factors of 10 using special- and general-purpose microprocessors. Electromechanical controllers can often cost five times more than a small processor system. Parts costs should also include the costs of support devices, such as the power supply of a system.

In considering a new product, the entire process should be examined for functions that could be assumed by a processor. Replacing a discrete fire alarm system with a processor system may be expensive. If other functions, the heating and security systems, are controlled by the same processor the overall savings may be great. In many systems the processor is relatively fast and has time to spare; put the processor to use in other applications and money is saved.

The flexibility of a micro system must be considered in any economic analysis. Changing system parameters or future system expansion can be easily accommodated by changing only the system software. A discrete controller might have to be junked when only a ROM would need replacing in a processor system. Auto ignition systems and programmable video games make good use of the ability of a processor system to change. From a basic manufacturing standpoint, one standard hardware board can be produced that will work well in a variety of applications when the proper software is supplied. It can even allow the customer to buy the board and develop his own software.

If a processor is to be included in a system the hardware/software breakdown must be performed. Functions must be assigned to either discrete hardware or system software. A list of all functions assumed by the processor allows the designer to consider the time requirements of each function individually and of all functions collectively. Interrupt prioritizing may be done with hardware if software prioritizing is too slow for peripherals. The time spent scanning a keyboard may be needed by another function, so a problem is solved by an externally encoded keyboard. Special function hardware chips, such as UARTS and math function calculators, can save a busy processor time and memory. Almost any function can, however, be performed with software. By balancing the fast and long functions with special hardware, a processor system can be made more efficient.

Assembling the hardware is an issue of importance. Motorola, AMI, and a host of consulting firms offer a line of preassembled boards ranging from simple single board systems to minicomputer-like systems. Buying the hardware assembled may be advantageous for small quantity projects, projects with immediate completion times or for designers inexperienced with processor hardware. Building hardware can be less expensive if the fabrication and testing facilities and personnel are immediately available. High volume projects can be much less expensive if done in house. A wide variety of hobbyest systems are also available.

Good software can be written by first examining the requirements, then planning the program. The general functions to be implemented in software should first be listed in a general flowchart. The order of performance and any special requirements of functions can be listed but details should not appear. Interrelationships can be noted on this chart. Each function is then flowcharted, written, run, and debugged separately. The completed functions are then assembled into the total program. Breaking a program into functions can make a large insurmountable-looking problem appear to be a series of smaller, manageable problems.

The 6800 microprocessor is a powerful yet easy to use machine that can be fun and fulfilling. You now have the basics of its hardware and software operation. Have fun in adapting the 6800 to your needs.

APPENDIX

Miscellaneous Information

MANUFACTURERS' ADDRESSES

Three manufacturers are currently producing 6800 products:

Motorola Semiconductor Products, Inc.
Box 20912
Phoenix, Arizona 85036

American Microsystems, Inc.
3800 Homestead Road
Santa Clara, California 95051

Fairchild Camera & Instrument Corp.
464 Ellis Street
Mountain View, California 94042

PROGRAMMER'S CARD

Motorola's programmer's card for the 6800 has been duplicated on pages 172 and 173 and on the card inside the back cover.

ACCUMULATOR AND MEMORY OPERATIONS	MNEMONIC	ADDRESSING MODES: IMMED			DIRECT			INDEX			EXTND			INHER			BOOLEAN/ARITHMETIC OPERATION (All register labels refer to contents)	COND. CODE REG.: 5	4	3	2	1	0
		OP	~	#	OP	~	#	OP	~	#	OP	~	#	OP	~	#		H	I	N	Z	V	C
Add	ADDA	8B	2	2	9B	3	2	AB	5	2	BB	4	3				A + M → A	↕	•	↕	↕	↕	↕
	ADDB	CB	2	2	DB	3	2	EB	5	2	FB	4	3				B + M → B	↕	•	↕	↕	↕	↕
Add Acmltrs	ABA													1B	2	1	A + B → A	↕	•	↕	↕	↕	↕
Add with Carry	ADCA	89	2	2	99	3	2	A9	5	2	B9	4	3				A + M + C → A	↕	•	↕	↕	↕	↕
	ADCB	C9	2	2	D9	3	2	E9	5	2	F9	4	3				B + M + C → B	↕	•	↕	↕	↕	↕
And	ANDA	84	2	2	94	3	2	A4	5	2	B4	4	3				A · M → A	•	•	↕	↕	R	•
	ANDB	C4	2	2	D4	3	2	E4	5	2	F4	4	3				B · M → B	•	•	↕	↕	R	•
Bit Test	BITA	85	2	2	95	3	2	A5	5	2	B5	4	3				A · M	•	•	↕	↕	R	•
	BITB	C5	2	2	D5	3	2	E5	5	2	F5	4	3				B · M	•	•	↕	↕	R	•
Clear	CLR							6F	7	2	7F	6	3				00 → M	•	•	R	S	R	R
	CLRA													4F	2	1	00 → A	•	•	R	S	R	R
	CLRB													5F	2	1	00 → B	•	•	R	S	R	R
Compare	CMPA	81	2	2	91	3	2	A1	5	2	B1	4	3				A − M	•	•	↕	↕	↕	↕
	CMPB	C1	2	2	D1	3	2	E1	5	2	F1	4	3				B − M	•	•	↕	↕	↕	↕
Compare Acmltrs	CBA													11	2	1	A − B	•	•	↕	↕	↕	↕
Complement, 1's	COM							63	7	2	73	6	3				$\bar{M}$ → M	•	•	↕	↕	R	S
	COMA													43	2	1	$\bar{A}$ → A	•	•	↕	↕	R	S
	COMB													53	2	1	$\bar{B}$ → B	•	•	↕	↕	R	S
Complement, 2's (Negate)	NEG							60	7	2	70	6	3				00 − M → M	•	•	↕	↕	①	②
	NEGA													40	2	1	00 − A → A	•	•	↕	↕	①	②
	NEGB													50	2	1	00 − B → B	•	•	↕	↕	①	②
Decimal Adjust, A	DAA													19	2	1	Converts Binary Add. of BCD Characters into BCD Format	•	•	↕	↕	↕	③
Decrement	DEC							6A	7	2	7A	6	3				M − 1 → M	•	•	↕	↕	④	•
	DECA													4A	2	1	A − 1 → A	•	•	↕	↕	④	•
	DECB													5A	2	1	B − 1 → B	•	•	↕	↕	④	•
Exclusive OR	EORA	88	2	2	98	3	2	A8	5	2	B8	4	3				A ⊕ M → A	•	•	↕	↕	R	•
	EORB	C8	2	2	D8	3	2	E8	5	2	F8	4	3				B ⊕ M → B	•	•	↕	↕	R	•
Increment	INC							6C	7	2	7C	6	3				M + 1 → M	•	•	↕	↕	⑤	•
	INCA													4C	2	1	A + 1 → A	•	•	↕	↕	⑤	•
	INCB													5C	2	1	B + 1 → B	•	•	↕	↕	⑤	•
Load Acmltr	LDAA	86	2	2	96	3	2	A6	5	2	B6	4	3				M → A	•	•	↕	↕	R	•
	LDAB	C6	2	2	D6	3	2	E6	5	2	F6	4	3				M → B	•	•	↕	↕	R	•
Or, Inclusive	ORAA	8A	2	2	9A	3	2	AA	5	2	BA	4	3				A + M → A	•	•	↕	↕	R	•
	ORAB	CA	2	2	DA	3	2	EA	5	2	FA	4	3				B + M → B	•	•	↕	↕	R	•
Push Data	PSHA													36	4	1	A → M_{SP}, SP − 1 → SP	•	•	•	•	•	•
	PSHB													37	4	1	B → M_{SP}, SP − 1 → SP	•	•	•	•	•	•
Pull Data	PULA													32	4	1	SP + 1 → SP, M_{SP} → A	•	•	•	•	•	•
	PULB													33	4	1	SP + 1 → SP, M_{SP} → B	•	•	•	•	•	•
Rotate Left	ROL							69	7	2	79	6	3				M	•	•	↕	↕	⑥	↕
	ROLA													49	2	1	A 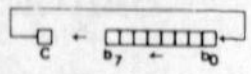	•	•	↕	↕	⑥	↕
	ROLB													59	2	1	B	•	•	↕	↕	⑥	↕
Rotate Right	ROR							66	7	2	76	6	3				M	•	•	↕	↕	⑥	↕
	RORA													46	2	1	A 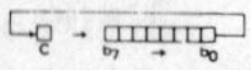	•	•	↕	↕	⑥	↕
	RORB													56	2	1	B	•	•	↕	↕	⑥	↕
Shift Left, Arithmetic	ASL							68	7	2	78	6	3				M	•	•	↕	↕	⑥	↕
	ASLA													48	2	1	A 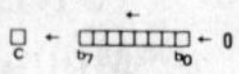	•	•	↕	↕	⑥	↕
	ASLB													58	2	1	B	•	•	↕	↕	⑥	↕
Shift Right, Arithmetic	ASR							67	7	2	77	6	3				M	•	•	↕	↕	⑥	↕
	ASRA													47	2	1	A 	•	•	↕	↕	⑥	↕
	ASRB													57	2	1	B	•	•	↕	↕	⑥	↕
Shift Right, Logic.	LSR							64	7	2	74	6	3				M	•	•	R	↕	⑥	↕
	LSRA													44	2	1	A 	•	•	R	↕	⑥	↕
	LSRB													54	2	1	B	•	•	R	↕	⑥	↕
Store Acmltr	STAA				97	4	2	A7	6	2	B7	5	3				A → M	•	•	↕	↕	R	•
	STAB				D7	4	2	E7	6	2	F7	5	3				B → M	•	•	↕	↕	R	•
Subtract	SUBA	80	2	2	90	3	2	A0	5	2	B0	4	3				A − M → A	•	•	↕	↕	↕	↕
	SUBB	C0	2	2	D0	3	2	E0	5	2	F0	4	3				B − M → B	•	•	↕	↕	↕	↕
Subract Acmltrs.	SBA													10	2	1	A − B → A	•	•	↕	↕	↕	↕
Subtr. with Carry	SBCA	82	2	2	92	3	2	A2	5	2	B2	4	3				A − M − C → A	•	•	↕	↕	↕	↕
	SBCB	C2	2	2	D2	3	2	E2	5	2	F2	4	3				B − M − C → B	•	•	↕	↕	↕	↕
Transfer Acmltrs	TAB													16	2	1	A → B	•	•	↕	↕	R	•
	TBA													17	2	1	B → A	•	•	↕	↕	R	•
Test, Zero or Minus	TST							6D	7	2	7D	6	3				M − 00	•	•	↕	↕	R	R
	TSTA													4D	2	1	A − 00	•	•	↕	↕	R	R
	TSTB													5D	2	1	B − 00	•	•	↕	↕	R	R

Courtesy Motorola Semiconductor Products, Inc.

INDEX REGISTER AND STACK POINTER OPERATIONS	MNEMONIC	IMMED OP	~	#	DIRECT OP	~	#	INDEX OP	~	#	EXTND OP	~	#	INHER OP	~	#	BOOLEAN/ARITHMETIC OPERATION	5 H	4 I	3 N	2 Z	1 V	0 C
Compare Index Reg	CPX	8C	3	3	9C	4	2	AC	6	2	BC	5	3				$(X_H/X_L) - (M/M+1)$	•	•	⑦	↕	⑧	•
Decrement Index Reg	DEX													09	4	1	$X - 1 \to X$	•	•	•	↕	•	•
Decrement Stack Pntr	DES													34	4	1	$SP - 1 \to SP$	•	•	•	•	•	•
Increment Index Reg	INX													08	4	1	$X + 1 \to X$	•	•	•	↕	•	•
Increment Stack Pntr	INS													31	4	1	$SP + 1 \to SP$	•	•	•	•	•	•
Load Index Reg	LDX	CE	3	3	DE	4	2	EE	6	2	FE	5	3				$M \to X_H, (M+1) \to X_L$	•	•	⑨	↕	R	•
Load Stack Pntr	LDS	8E	3	3	9E	4	2	AE	6	2	BE	5	3				$M \to SP_H, (M+1) \to SP_L$	•	•	⑨	↕	R	•
Store Index Reg	STX				DF	5	2	EF	7	2	FF	6	3				$X_H \to M, X_L \to (M+1)$	•	•	⑨	↕	R	•
Store Stack Pntr	STS				9F	5	2	AF	7	2	BF	6	3				$SP_H \to M, SP_L \to (M+1)$	•	•	⑨	↕	R	•
Indx Reg → Stack Pntr	TXS													35	4	1	$X - 1 \to SP$	•	•	•	•	•	•
Stack Pntr → Indx Reg	TSX													30	4	1	$SP + 1 \to X$	•	•	•	•	•	•

JUMP AND BRANCH OPERATIONS	MNEMONIC	RELATIVE OP	~	#	INDEX OP	~	#	EXTND OP	~	#	INHER OP	~	#	BRANCH TEST	5 H	4 I	3 N	2 Z	1 V	0 C
Branch Always	BRA	20	4	2										None	•	•	•	•	•	•
Branch If Carry Clear	BCC	24	4	2										$C = 0$	•	•	•	•	•	•
Branch If Carry Set	BCS	25	4	2										$C = 1$	•	•	•	•	•	•
Branch If = Zero	BEQ	27	4	2										$Z = 1$	•	•	•	•	•	•
Branch If ≥ Zero	BGE	2C	4	2										$N \oplus V = 0$	•	•	•	•	•	•
Branch If > Zero	BGT	2E	4	2										$Z + (N \oplus V) = 0$	•	•	•	•	•	•
Branch If Higher	BHI	22	4	2										$C + Z = 0$	•	•	•	•	•	•
Branch If ≤ Zero	BLE	2F	4	2										$Z + (N \oplus V) = 1$	•	•	•	•	•	•
Branch If Lower Or Same	BLS	23	4	2										$C + Z = 1$	•	•	•	•	•	•
Branch If < Zero	BLT	2D	4	2										$N \oplus V = 1$	•	•	•	•	•	•
Branch If Minus	BMI	2B	4	2										$N = 1$	•	•	•	•	•	•
Branch If Not Equal Zero	BNE	26	4	2										$Z = 0$	•	•	•	•	•	•
Branch If Overflow Clear	BVC	28	4	2										$V = 0$	•	•	•	•	•	•
Branch If Overflow Set	BVS	29	4	2										$V = 1$	•	•	•	•	•	•
Branch If Plus	BPL	2A	4	2										$N = 0$	•	•	•	•	•	•
Branch To Subroutine	BSR	8D	8	2										See Special Operations	•	•	•	•	•	•
Jump	JMP				6E	4	2	7E	3	3				See Special Operations	•	•	•	•	•	•
Jump To Subroutine	JSR				AD	8	2	BD	9	3				See Special Operations	•	•	•	•	•	•
No Operation	NOP										01	2	1	Advances Prog. Cntr. Only	•	•	•	•	•	•
Return From Interrupt	RTI										3B	10	1		⑩					
Return From Subroutine	RTS										39	5	1	See special Operations	•	•	•	•	•	•
Software Interrupt	SWI										3F	12	1	See special Operations	•	S	•	•	•	•
Wait for Interrupt	WAI										3E	9	1	See special Operations	•	⑪	•	•	•	•

CONDITIONS CODE REGISTER OPERATIONS	MNEMONIC	INHER OP	~	=	BOOLEAN OPERATION	5 H	4 I	3 N	2 Z	1 V	0 C
Clear Carry	CLC	0C	2	1	$0 \to C$	•	•	•	•	•	R
Clear Interrupt Mask	CLI	0E	2	1	$0 \to I$	•	R	•	•	•	•
Clear Overflow	CLV	0A	2	1	$0 \to V$	•	•	•	•	R	•
Set Carry	SEC	0D	2	1	$1 \to C$	•	•	•	•	•	S
Set Interrupt Mask	SEI	0F	2	1	$1 \to I$	•	S	•	•	•	•
Set Overflow	SEV	0B	2	1	$1 \to V$	•	•	•	•	S	•
Acmltr A → CCR	TAP	06	2	1	$A \to CCR$	⑫					
CCR → Acmltr A	TPA	07	2	1	$CCR \to A$	•	•	•	•	•	•

CONDITION CODE REGISTER NOTES:

(Bit set if test is true and cleared otherwise)

① (Bit V) Test: Result = 10000000?
② (Bit C) Test: Result = 00000000?
③ (Bit C) Test: Decimal value of most significant BCD Character greater than nine? (Not cleared if previously set.)
④ (Bit V) Test: Operand = 10000000 prior to execution?
⑤ (Bit V) Test: Operand = 01111111 prior to execution?
⑥ (Bit V) Test: Set equal to result of N ⊕ C after shift has occurred.
⑦ (Bit N) Test: Sign bit of most significant (MS) byte of result = 1?
⑧ (Bit V) Test: 2's complement overflow from subtraction of LS bytes?
⑨ (Bit N) Test: Result less than zero? (Bit 15 = 1)
⑩ (All) Load Condition Code Register from Stack. (See Special Operations)
⑪ (Bit I) Set when interrupt occurs. If previously set, a Non-Maskable Interrupt is required to exit the wait state.
⑫ (ALL) Set according to the contents of Accumulator A.

LEGEND:

OP	Operation Code (Hexadecimal);	00	Byte = Zero;
~	Number of MPU Cycles;	H	Half-carry from bit 3;
#	Number of Program Bytes;	I	Interrupt mask
+	Arithmetic Plus;	N	Negative (sign bit)
–	Arithmetic Minus;	Z	Zero (byte)
•	Boolean AND;	V	Overflow, 2's complement
M_{SP}	Contents of memory location pointed to be Stack Pointer;	C	Carry from bit 7
		R	Reset Always
		S	Set Always
+	Boolean Inclusive OR;	↕	Test and set if true, cleared otherwise
⊕	Boolean Exclusive OR;	•	Not Affected
$\overline{M}$	Complement of M;	CCR	Condition Code Register
→	Transfer Into;	LS	Least Significant
0	Bit = Zero;	MS	Most Significant

Courtesy Motorola Semiconductor Products, Inc.

Index

ACCUMULATOR AND MEMORY OPERATIONS	MNEMONIC	IMMED OP	IMMED ~	IMMED #	DIRECT OP	DIRECT ~	DIRECT #	INDEX OP	INDEX ~	INDEX #	EXTND OP	EXTND ~	EXTND #	INHER OP	INHER ~	INHER #	BOOLEAN/ARITHMETIC OPERATION (All register labels refer to contents)	5 H	4 I	3 N	2 Z	1 V	0 C
Add	ADDA	8B	2	2	9B	3	2	AB	5	2	BB	4	3				A + M → A	↕	•	↕	↕	↕	↕
	ADDB	CB	2	2	DB	3	2	EB	5	2	FB	4	3				B + M → B	↕	•	↕	↕	↕	↕
Add Acmltrs	ABA													1B	2	1	A + B → A	↕	•	↕	↕	↕	↕
Add with Carry	ADCA	89	2	2	99	3	2	A9	5	2	B9	4	3				A + M + C → A	↕	•	↕	↕	↕	↕
	ADCB	C9	2	2	D9	3	2	E9	5	2	F9	4	3				B + M + C → B	↕	•	↕	↕	↕	↕
And	ANDA	84	2	2	94	3	2	A4	5	2	B4	4	3				A • M → A	•	•	↕	↕	R	•
	ANDB	C4	2	2	D4	3	2	E4	5	2	F4	4	3				B • M → B	•	•	↕	↕	R	•
Bit Test	BITA	85	2	2	95	3	2	A5	5	2	B5	4	3				A • M	•	•	↕	↕	R	•
	BITB	C5	2	2	D5	3	2	E5	5	2	F5	4	3				B • M	•	•	↕	↕	R	•
Clear	CLR							6F	7	2	7F	6	3				00 → M	•	•	R	S	R	R
	CLRA													4F	2	1	00 → A	•	•	R	S	R	R
	CLRB													5F	2	1	00 → B	•	•	R	S	R	R
Compare	CMPA	81	2	2	91	3	2	A1	5	2	B1	4	3				A − M	•	•	↕	↕	↕	↕
	CMPB	C1	2	2	D1	3	2	E1	5	2	F1	4	3				B − M	•	•	↕	↕	↕	↕
Compare Acmltrs	CBA													11	2	1	A − B	•	•	↕	↕	↕	↕
Complement, 1's	COM							63	7	2	73	6	3				$\overline{M}$ → M	•	•	↕	↕	R	S
	COMA													43	2	1	$\overline{A}$ → A	•	•	↕	↕	R	S
	COMB													53	2	1	$\overline{B}$ → B	•	•	↕	↕	R	S
Complement, 2's (Negate)	NEG							60	7	2	70	6	3				00 − M → M	•	•	↕	↕	①	②
	NEGA													40	2	1	00 − A → A	•	•	↕	↕	①	②
	NEGB													50	2	1	00 − B → B	•	•	↕	↕	①	②
Decimal Adjust, A	DAA													19	2	1	Converts Binary Add. of BCD Characters into BCD Format	•	•	↕	↕	↕	③
Decrement	DEC							6A	7	2	7A	6	3				M − 1 → M	•	•	↕	↕	④	•
	DECA													4A	2	1	A − 1 → A	•	•	↕	↕	④	•
	DECB													5A	2	1	B − 1 → B	•	•	↕	↕	④	•
Exclusive OR	EORA	88	2	2	98	3	2	A8	5	2	B8	4	3				A ⊕ M → A	•	•	↕	↕	R	•
	EORB	C8	2	2	D8	3	2	E8	5	2	F8	4	3				B ⊕ M → B	•	•	↕	↕	R	•
Increment	INC							6C	7	2	7C	6	3				M + 1 → M	•	•	↕	↕	⑤	•
	INCA													4C	2	1	A + 1 → A	•	•	↕	↕	⑤	•
	INCB													5C	2	1	B + 1 → B	•	•	↕	↕	⑤	•
Load Acmltr	LDAA	86	2	2	96	3	2	A6	5	2	B6	4	3				M → A	•	•	↕	↕	R	•
	LDAB	C6	2	2	D6	3	2	E6	5	2	F6	4	3				M → B	•	•	↕	↕	R	•
Or, Inclusive	ORAA	8A	2	2	9A	3	2	AA	5	2	BA	4	3				A + M → A	•	•	↕	↕	R	•
	ORAB	CA	2	2	DA	3	2	EA	5	2	FA	4	3				B + M → B	•	•	↕	↕	R	•
Push Data	PSHA													36	4	1	A → M_{SP}, SP − 1 → SP	•	•	•	•	•	•
	PSHB													37	4	1	B → M_{SP}, SP − 1 → SP	•	•	•	•	•	•
Pull Data	PULA													32	4	1	SP + 1 → SP, M_{SP} → A	•	•	•	•	•	•
	PULB													33	4	1	SP + 1 → SP, M_{SP} → B	•	•	•	•	•	•
Rotate Left	ROL							69	7	2	79	6	3				M	•	•	↕	↕	⑥	↕
	ROLA													49	2	1	A 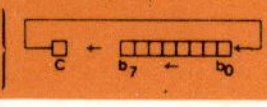	•	•	↕	↕	⑥	↕
	ROLB													59	2	1	B	•	•	↕	↕	⑥	↕
Rotate Right	ROR							66	7	2	76	6	3				M	•	•	↕	↕	⑥	↕
	RORA													46	2	1	A 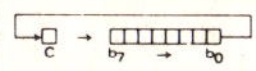	•	•	↕	↕	⑥	↕
	RORB													56	2	1	B	•	•	↕	↕	⑥	↕
Shift Left, Arithmetic	ASL							68	7	2	78	6	3				M	•	•	↕	↕	⑥	↕
	ASLA													48	2	1	A 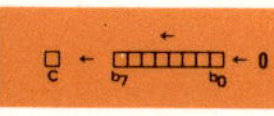	•	•	↕	↕	⑥	↕
	ASLB													58	2	1	B	•	•	↕	↕	⑥	↕
Shift Right, Arithmetic	ASR							67	7	2	77	6	3				M	•	•	↕	↕	⑥	↕
	ASRA													47	2	1	A 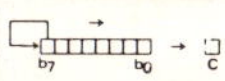	•	•	↕	↕	⑥	↕
	ASRB													57	2	1	B	•	•	↕	↕	⑥	↕
Shift Right, Logic.	LSR							64	7	2	74	6	3				M	•	•	R	↕	⑥	↕
	LSRA													44	2	1	A 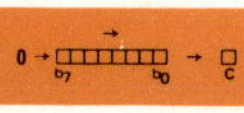	•	•	R	↕	⑥	↕
	LSRB													54	2	1	B	•	•	R	↕	⑥	↕
Store Acmltr.	STAA				97	4	2	A7	6	2	B7	5	3				A → M	•	•	↕	↕	R	•
	STAB				D7	4	2	E7	6	2	F7	5	3				B → M	•	•	↕	↕	R	•
Subtract	SUBA	80	2	2	90	3	2	A0	5	2	B0	4	3				A − M → A	•	•	↕	↕	↕	↕
	SUBB	C0	2	2	D0	3	2	E0	5	2	F0	4	3				B − M → B	•	•	↕	↕	↕	↕
Subract Acmltrs.	SBA													10	2	1	A − B → A	•	•	↕	↕	↕	↕
Subtr. with Carry	SBCA	82	2	2	92	3	2	A2	5	2	B2	4	3				A − M − C → A	•	•	↕	↕	↕	↕
	SBCB	C2	2	2	D2	3	2	E2	5	2	F2	4	3				B − M − C → B	•	•	↕	↕	↕	↕
Transfer Acmltrs	TAB													16	2	1	A → B	•	•	↕	↕	R	•
	TBA													17	2	1	B → A	•	•	↕	↕	R	•
Test, Zero or Minus	TST							6D	7	2	7D	6	3				M − 00	•	•	↕	↕	R	R
	TSTA													4D	2	1	A − 00	•	•	↕	↕	R	R
	TSTB													5D	2	1	B − 00	•	•	↕	↕	R	R

INDEX REGISTER AND STACK POINTER OPERATIONS	MNEMONIC	IMMED OP	IMMED ~	IMMED #	DIRECT OP	DIRECT ~	DIRECT #	INDEX OP	INDEX ~	INDEX #	EXTND OP	EXTND ~	EXTND #	INHER OP	INHER ~	INHER #	BOOLEAN/ARITHMETIC OPERATION	5 H	4 I	3 N	2 Z	1 V	0 C
Compare Index Reg	CPX	8C	3	3	9C	4	2	AC	6	2	BC	5	3				$(X_H/X_L) - (M/M+1)$	•	•	(7)	↕	(8)	•
Decrement Index Reg	DEX													09	4	1	$X - 1 \rightarrow X$	•	•	•	↕	•	•
Decrement Stack Pntr	DES													34	4	1	$SP - 1 \rightarrow SP$	•	•	•	•	•	•
Increment Index Reg	INX													08	4	1	$X + 1 \rightarrow X$	•	•	•	↕	•	•
Increment Stack Pntr	INS													31	4	1	$SP + 1 \rightarrow SP$	•	•	•	•	•	•
Load Index Reg	LDX	CE	3	3	DE	4	2	EE	6	2	FE	5	3				$M \rightarrow X_H, (M+1) \rightarrow X_L$	•	•	(9)	↕	R	•
Load Stack Pntr	LDS	8E	3	3	9E	4	2	AE	6	2	BE	5	3				$M \rightarrow SP_H, (M+1) \rightarrow SP_L$	•	•	(9)	↕	R	•
Store Index Reg	STX				DF	5	2	EF	7	2	FF	6	3				$X_H \rightarrow M, X_L \rightarrow (M+1)$	•	•	(9)	↕	R	•
Store Stack Pntr	STS				9F	5	2	AF	7	2	BF	6	3				$SP_H \rightarrow M, SP_L \rightarrow (M+1)$	•	•	(9)	↕	R	•
Indx Reg → Stack Pntr	TXS													35	4	1	$X - 1 \rightarrow SP$	•	•	•	•	•	•
Stack Pntr → Indx Reg	TSX													30	4	1	$SP + 1 \rightarrow X$	•	•	•	•	•	•

JUMP AND BRANCH OPERATIONS	MNEMONIC	RELATIVE OP	RELATIVE ~	RELATIVE #	INDEX OP	INDEX ~	INDEX #	EXTND OP	EXTND ~	EXTND #	INHER OP	INHER ~	INHER #	BRANCH TEST	5 H	4 I	3 N	2 Z	1 V	0 C
Branch Always	BRA	20	4	2										None	•	•	•	•	•	•
Branch If Carry Clear	BCC	24	4	2										$C = 0$	•	•	•	•	•	•
Branch If Carry Set	BCS	25	4	2										$C = 1$	•	•	•	•	•	•
Branch If = Zero	BEQ	27	4	2										$Z = 1$	•	•	•	•	•	•
Branch If ≥ Zero	BGE	2C	4	2										$N \oplus V = 0$	•	•	•	•	•	•
Branch If > Zero	BGT	2E	4	2										$Z + (N \oplus V) = 0$	•	•	•	•	•	•
Branch If Higher	BHI	22	4	2										$C + Z = 0$	•	•	•	•	•	•
Branch If ≤ Zero	BLE	2F	4	2										$Z + (N \oplus V) = 1$	•	•	•	•	•	•
Branch If Lower Or Same	BLS	23	4	2										$C + Z = 1$	•	•	•	•	•	•
Branch If < Zero	BLT	2D	4	2										$N \oplus V = 1$	•	•	•	•	•	•
Branch If Minus	BMI	2B	4	2										$N = 1$	•	•	•	•	•	•
Branch If Not Equal Zero	BNE	26	4	2										$Z = 0$	•	•	•	•	•	•
Branch If Overflow Clear	BVC	28	4	2										$V = 0$	•	•	•	•	•	•
Branch If Overflow Set	BVS	29	4	2										$V = 1$	•	•	•	•	•	•
Branch If Plus	BPL	2A	4	2										$N = 0$	•	•	•	•	•	•
Branch To Subroutine	BSR	8D	8	2										See Special Operations	•	•	•	•	•	•
Jump	JMP				6E	4	2	7E	3	3				See Special Operations	•	•	•	•	•	•
Jump To Subroutine	JSR				AD	8	2	BD	9	3				See Special Operations	•	•	•	•	•	•
No Operation	NOP										01	2	1	Advances Prog. Cntr. Only	•	•	•	•	•	•
Return From Interrupt	RTI										3B	10	1	See special Operations	(10)					
Return From Subroutine	RTS										39	5	1	See special Operations	•	•	•	•	•	•
Software Interrupt	SWI										3F	12	1	See special Operations	•	S	•	•	•	•
Wait for Interrupt	WAI										3E	9	1	See special Operations	•	(11)	•	•	•	•

CONDITIONS CODE REGISTER OPERATIONS	MNEMONIC	INHER OP	INHER ~	INHER #	BOOLEAN OPERATION	5 H	4 I	3 N	2 Z	1 V	0 C
Clear Carry	CLC	0C	2	1	$0 \rightarrow C$	•	•	•	•	•	R
Clear Interrupt Mask	CLI	0E	2	1	$0 \rightarrow I$	•	R	•	•	•	•
Clear Overflow	CLV	0A	2	1	$0 \rightarrow V$	•	•	•	•	R	•
Set Carry	SEC	0D	2	1	$1 \rightarrow C$	•	•	•	•	•	S
Set Interrupt Mask	SEI	0F	2	1	$1 \rightarrow I$	•	S	•	•	•	•
Set Overflow	SEV	0B	2	1	$1 \rightarrow V$	•	•	•	•	S	•
Acmltr A → CCR	TAP	06	2	1	$A \rightarrow CCR$	(12)					
CCR → Acmltr A	TPA	07	2	1	$CCR \rightarrow A$	•	•	•	•	•	•

CONDITION CODE REGISTER NOTES:

(Bit set if test is true and cleared otherwise)

1. (Bit V) Test: Result = 10000000?
2. (Bit C) Test: Result = 00000000?
3. (Bit C) Test: Decimal value of most significant BCD Character greater than nine? (Not cleared if previously set.)
4. (Bit V) Test: Operand = 10000000 prior to execution?
5. (Bit V) Test: Operand = 01111111 prior to execution?
6. (Bit V) Test: Set equal to result of $N \oplus C$ after shift has occurred.
7. (Bit N) Test: Sign bit of most significant (MS) byte of result = 1?
8. (Bit V) Test: 2's complement overflow from subtraction of LS bytes?
9. (Bit N) Test: Result less than zero? (Bit 15 = 1)
10. (All) Load Condition Code Register from Stack. (See Special Operations)
11. (Bit I) Set when interrupt occurs. If previously set, a Non-Maskable Interrupt is required to exit the wait state.
12. (ALL) Set according to the contents of Accumulator A.

LEGEND:

OP	Operation Code (Hexadecimal);	00	Byte = Zero;
~	Number of MPU Cycles;	H	Half-carry from bit 3;
#	Number of Program Bytes;	I	Interrupt mask
+	Arithmetic Plus;	N	Negative (sign bit)
–	Arithmetic Minus;	Z	Zero (byte)
•	Boolean AND;	V	Overflow, 2's complement
M_{SP}	Contents of memory location pointed to be Stack Pointer;	C	Carry from bit 7
+	Boolean Inclusive OR;	R	Reset Always
⊕	Boolean Exclusive OR;	S	Set Always
$\overline{M}$	Complement of M;	↕	Test and set if true, cleared otherwise
→	Transfer Into;	•	Not Affected
0	Bit = Zero;	CCR	Condition Code Register
		LS	Least Significant
		MS	Most Significant